LECTURES ON COMPARATIVE RELIGION

LECTURES ON COMPARATIVE RELIGION

STEPHANOS NIRMALENDU LECTURES

BY

ARTHUR ANTHONY MACDONELL, M.A.
(OXON.)
PH.D. (LEIPZIG), HON. D. LITT. (EDIN.), D.O.L. (CAI).
BONDEN PROFESSOR OF SANSKRIT IN THE UNIVERSITY
OF OXFORD AND FELLOW OF BALLIOL COLLEGE,
OXFORD

GYAN

Published by

Gyan Publishing House
5, Ansari Road
Daryaganj, New Delhi-110002
Phone: 011-47034999, 9811692060
E-mail: books@gyanbooks.com

Distribution Network
gyanbooks.com
India, USA, Canada, UK, Australia, France

ISBN : 978-81-212-2536-6 (HB)
First Published, 1925

2nd Impression 2021

Printed at: Gyan Press, Delhi.

Lectures on Comparative Religion
Author: Arthur Anthony Macdonell

LECTURES ON COMPARATIVE RELIGION

STEPHANOS NIRMALENDU LECTURES

BY

ARTHUR ANTHONY MACDONELL, M.A. (Oxon.),
Ph.D. (Leipzig), Hon. D.Litt. (Edin.), D.O.L. (Cal.),
Boden Professor of Sanskrit in the University of Oxford
and Fellow of Balliol College, Oxford

PUBLISHED BY THE
UNIVERSITY OF CALCUTTA
1925

CONTENTS

LECTURES ON COMPARATIVE RELIGION

LECTURE I

A. Introduction

Mr. Vice-Chancellor and Gentlemen,

Before beginning the actual course of lectures which I have undertaken to deliver before you for the Stephanos Nirmalendu Ghosh foundation, I think it will interest you if, by way of personal introduction, I make a few statements about my relations to India as a country and to the study of India's ancient language and literature. Though both my father and my mother were natives of the North of Scotland, at the western geographical limit of the Indo-European nations, I myself was born in the north-east of India, their oriental frontier. For I first saw the light at Mozuffarpur in Tirhut more than sixty years ago. All the impressions and recollections of the first seven years of my life go back to Indian scenes, with Indian trees, fruits, and flowers, Indian animals, birds, and reptiles, Indian bungalows, camps, and bazaars, and lastly many kind Indian servants. I remember the Himālaya, the Ganges and its tributary the Gandak, Pusa (now an Agricultural College), Sonpur, Buxar, Patna, Mussoorie, and finally Calcutta, to which I came down the Ganges with my parents in a houseboat. I have still a vivid recollection of a scene at Calcutta, when I fell into a tank while helping another boy to push off the model of a sailing ship from one of the steps leading down to the water. My last recollection of India from my childhood is of the day on which my father, who was an officer in the Army, took leave of us on board a large sailing ship named the Agamemnon, in the Hooghly, before we started on the voyage to London. This parting scene has always remained in my memory as illustrating a sad phase of the life of Europeans in India. I may add that my mother had seven brothers and sisters in India, most of them at the same time as herself; and that my father and three uncles lie buried in Indian soil. Thus you see that as far as family ties are concerned my early connexion with India was very intimate. But later on, it became even closer intellectually, for in that sense it has lasted forty-seven years. During the six years before I came up to Oxford as an undergraduate, I was educated at the public school and the University of Göttingen in Germany. As soon as I matriculated at Göttingen early in 1875, I began the study of Sanskrit and Comparative Philology under Professor Theodore Benfey, one of the four great pioneers of Vedic studies in Europe, and the editor in 1848 of the *Sāmaveda*, the first of the four Vedas to be critically published in its entirety. After coming up to Oxford in 1876, I continued my Sanskrit studies under Professor Monier Williams and gained the Boden Sanskrit Scholarship. While still an undergraduate I taught Sanskrit to Bunyiu Nanjio, the first Japanese to study Sanskrit in modern times, and now a noted Buddhist preacher in Japan. When I had taken my degree at Oxford, I continued my Vedic studies under the guidance of Professor Max Müller, the first editor of the *Rigveda*, and began preparing to publish an edition of the *Sarvānukramaṇī* an early Index to the RV. This came out in 1886. I also took the opportunity of deepening my Vedic knowledge under the stimulus of Professor Roth at the University of Tübingen in Germany. He was a great Vedic scholar, being the joint editor with the American Sanskritist, Professor Whitney, of the *Atharvaveda*, as well as the compiler, in collaboration with Dr. Böhtlingk, of the Vedic part of the great St. Petersburg Sanskrit Dictionary, a work that has contributed more than any other to the critical investigation of the ancient language and literature of India. I further went on to the University of Leipzig, where nearly forty years ago I took the degree of Ph.D. with a Vedic text as my thesis and Comparative Philology and Old German as secondary subjects of examination. It was the mixture of Scotch parentage, Indian birth, German education, together with the study of Sanskrit and of Comparative Philology which led an old college friend, even in my undergraduate days, to describe me summarily as an "Indo-Germanic Scot."

In 1884 I first began to teach Sanskrit officially to the Indian Civil Service Probationers at Balliol College. Among the pupils of that year was included Edward Maclagan, now Governor of the Panjab; a few years later came Nicholas Beatson-Bell, John Ghest Cumming, C. A. Oldham, the late Professor Das Gupta, and a good many others who have been well known in this Presidency. In 1888 I became Deputy Professor of Sanskrit on the retirement of Sir M. Monier-Williams, and after his death in 1899, I was elected to the full Boden Professorship of Sanskrit, which I continue to hold. In 1907 I was granted leave by the University of Oxford for two terms, in order to make a tour of study and research in India, an opportunity I had been longing for during many years, and was now at last enabled to carry out. The purpose of this tour, for which I had carefully prepared myself, was to examine the archæological remains in all parts of the country, as illustrating the history of the Indian religions, Buddhism, Jainism, and Hinduism. This object I fully accomplished. I took many photographs and obtained many others from the Archæological department. Thus after my return I was able to give many lectures on the religions of India, illustrated by numerous lantern slides, in Oxford, London, Aberdeen,

St. Andrews and other places. These lectures aroused a good deal of interest, not only among British audiences, but also among Indian students, few of whom had any idea of the archæological treasures that India contains, still less of their value in the interpretation of bygone phases of Indian religion. Archæological research is peculiarly important in India, because, owing to the great lack of directly historical documents, antiquarian remains, including coins, are for early times almost the only historical evidence we possess.

Among the secondary objects I had in view was the acquisition of Sanskrit MSS. With the aid of Mahāmahopādhyāya Haraprasād Śāstrī I came across in Benares a valuable private collection of between 6,000 and 7,000 Sanskrit MSS. The owner, who wished to sell the collection, gave me the refusal of it till I should have returned to Oxford. The result was that the Mahārāja Prime Minister of Nepāl, purchased the MSS. and presented them to the Bodleian at Oxford, which is the largest University Library in the world. These MSS. have been classified, handlisted, and to a considerable extent bound by this time. A good many of them have already been examined or collated by Sanskrit scholars, including several of my own pupils. Taken altogether, there are about 10,000 Sanskrit MSS. at Oxford, more than in all the Western libraries put together. It is therefore likely that this will become the chief centre for the collation of Sanskrit MSS. in the West, both because of their number and the select character of several of the collections.

My literary Sanskrit career began about 36 years ago in 1886, when I published my edition of the *Sarvānukramaṇī* of the *Ṛigveda*, besides a new and abridged edition of Max Müller's *Sanskrit Grammar for Beginners*. This was followed by a Sanskrit-English Dictionary in 1892. I had begun to specialize more and more on the Veda; partly because of the influence of the three great Vedic scholars of whom I had been the pupil, and partly because no British scholar had taken up this phase of ancient Indian literature, though it is both linguistically and historically the most important. There was, moreover, in every country a conspicuous lack of books adapted to the wants of the student of the subject. I therefore began to bring out books dealing with the Vedas mainly from the learner's point of-view. The first work of this kind was my *Vedic Mythology* published in 1897. This was a complete critical treatment of the subject based throughout on the direct evidence of the Vedic texts. Then came in 1900 the *History of Sanskrit Literature*, the greater part of which deals with the Vedic period. The publication in 1904 of the text and translation of the *Bṛhaddevatā*, which deals with the gods of the *Rigveda*, was followed in 1910 by my large *Vedic Grammar*, which was published in Germany. This work, which embodies the results of many years of hard work, for the first time presented all the grammatical material contained in Vedic texts. In 1912 appeared the *Vedic Index of Names and Subjects*, which was produced in collaboration with my former pupil, Dr. A. Berriedale Keith, now Regius Professor of Sanskrit and Comparative Philology at Edinburgh University. This book embraces practically all the historical material contained in the Vedic texts. Four years later (1916) came my *Vedic Grammar for Students*, which while leaving out many details contained in the large grammar, adds new matter on syntax and metre. Next year (1917) I published a *Vedic Reader*, which supplies a representative selection of the hymns of the *Rigveda*, accompanied by notes explaining every point, so that the student working by himself can, with the additional help of the *Vedic Grammar*, become an independent Vedic scholar. This book I undertook especially for the purpose of increasing the number of genuine Vedic students, in the absence of any appreciable number of competent teachers of the subject. Last year I published a long and detailed article on *Vedic Religion* in the form of an Encyclopædia article. Finally, I have completed a selection of Vedic hymns metrically translated into verse that is as near the original metre as possible. This work has been printed at Calcutta during the present year, and has been published within the last few days. It is only a forerunner of a critical prose translation of the *Rigveda* for which my studies during more than thirty years have been a preparation, of which I have already completed an appreciable part, and which I hope to bring to a conclusion by the end of my life. If this purpose shall have been accomplished, my career, which began with India in one sense, will thus close with India in another. I trust that my life's work will then have contributed something, as far as India at least is concerned, to the enlargement of the frontiers of knowledge, and by thus increasing enlightenment, help, in some small degree, to promote the advancement of humanity.

The scientific and critical study of the *Rigveda* has in the latter half of the 19th and the first twenty years of the present century already done much to widen the horizon of civilized mankind. For this, the earliest record of a religion which can be studied historically for more than 3,000 years, led to the foundation of a new science, one of the evidences for the importance of which, is the 50 volumes of the *Sacred Books of the East*, published by the Clarendon Press at Oxford, and another is the existence of several chairs to represent it in the universities of different countries. I mean the science of Comparative Religion.

The subject of the present course of lectures comes within the range of this science, which by removing a vast mass of prejudice, is bound, perhaps more than any other study, to help forward enlightenment and tolerance among mankind. According to the wishes of the founder of this lectureship, it should be the aim of the Lecturer to show that the highest ideal for man is to be found in unselfish love and service of his fellows which is the essence of the teachings of Christ. He does not desire his young countrymen to be taught that man's eternal welfare should depend on any particular form of belief, the interpretation of a particular text, or the acceptance of a religious creed, but that rather the love and service of his fellow beings should be the guiding principle of his life; that considering the extent to which, in the past, the persecuting spirit has entered into most forms of religious belief, it ought to be shown rather that living the religion of love constitutes the highest development of man's personality. With this view I may say I am in thorough sympathy. In some western universities it is the custom to appoint laymen to chairs of theology, because a clergyman cannot, however fair-minded he be, avoid a certain bias, at least as far as his own religion or sect is concerned. In the present case, I hold the position of such a layman: though brought up in the atmosphere of Christianity, the general spirit of which I have imbibed, I do not hold a brief for any particular dogma. Towards the different religions that I propose to pass in review, my attitude will be that of a judge, not of an advocate; or that of the scholar, whose guiding star is the search for truth.

There have been a great many definitions of religion: it would be waste of time to discuss all these here. I will content myself with repeating the definition which I gave twenty-five years ago in my *Vedic Mythology* as 'the conception which men entertain of the divine or supernatural powers, and that sense of the dependence of human welfare on those powers which finds its expression in various forms of worship.' While religion is, strictly speaking, the relation of man to the divine powers, and morality concerns man's relation to his neighbour, the two spheres of religion and morality have become entirely separated as subjects of scientific treatment in quite modern times only. In the past, they have been inseparably intermingled in varying degrees, as is illustrated by the sense of the Sanskrit word *dharma* which means 'divine and moral law.' This word includes *ācāra* 'conduct,' which resembles in sense the English word 'morality' as derived from the Latin *mores*, 'habits,' 'custom.'

In practice morality has always been under the sanction of religion, that is to say, moral conduct has been enforced by the penalties or rewards imposed by religion. We see this union in most of the sacred books of the various ancient religions, as in the Jewish Old Testament, in the Arabic Quran, and in the Indian Vedas, or even in what are specifically called Lawbooks (*dharmaśāstra*).

In the earliest religions the sphere of morality was at first very narrow, being of an egoistical character, and embracing only a man's person and his immediate belongings, that is, his family ; it then gradually grew to include the kin-group or the clan ; then the nation or amalgamation of tribes, conscious of a common racial descent, and having common language, religion, and customs. Within these progressive bounds was developed a gradual advance from egoism to justice, and even in a certain degree to altruism, but beyond these national limits in most ancient religions all outsiders were regarded as potential enemies, to whom the claims of the national morality did not extend. Thus beyond the pale of Judaism were the gentiles, of Hellenism the barbarians, of the Indo-Aryans the Dāsas or Mlecchas ; of the Chinese the foreign devils ; of the Moslems the Kaffirs. This attitude towards outsiders has in some cases lasted down to the present day ; in the remaining cases outsiders are only foreigners, towards whom, however, a lower standard of right and justice is still considered sufficient, as for instance, in the sphere of prices. Thus, when I first travelled in the German part of Switzerland, I found there were three grades of prices : the lowest for the native Swiss, the next for the Germans, and the highest for the English and Americans. Progressive morality has as yet by no means arrived at the standard of conduct in which nations should treat each other by the same rules as those which prevail among individuals. It is true that in recent centuries there has gradually come into existence a code of international law by which disputes between nations are to be decided according to justice and equity; but this agreement entirely broke down in the late world-war, because one of the two groups of belligerents proved that the sole standard by which they were guided in their political dealings with other nations was force and not right. Had that group been victorious, it is not too much to say that the moral standard of world-civilization would have moved backward by several centuries. The result of that titanic struggle encourages us to believe that civilization is destined to progress, and that right will ultimately prove the guiding star of all mankind. It is true that, as we shall see, some of the leading thinkers of antiquity more than 2,000 years ago had advanced to the conception of the brotherhood of mankind, and that at the present day the religion which has spread farthest over the surface of the earth, embraces the whole of humanity as on an equal footing; but ethical practice is still far from realizing this religious ideal.

All the leading religions have arisen in the East: in this sense the Latin motto of the Royal Asiatic Society of Great Britain, *ex oriente lux*, 'light comes from the orient,' is applicable to them. The two oldest of them, the Egyptian and the Assyrian, ceased to exist in antiquity, but have left records that enable us to know their character in some detail. The eight that survive are either national or world religions, the literary records of which go back either to the time when they arose or were founded, or at any rate to near that time. All these ten religions have been produced by three of the great divisions of mankind: by the Chinese, the Aryans, and the Semites. The Chinese originated one of them: Confucianism, which has remained the chief religion of that people for 2,500 years and is professed by about 300,000,000 adherents. The Aryans produced four. One of these, Zoroastrianism, the ancient religion of Persia, which in various respects is very closely allied to the faith of the Vedic Aryans, was almost entirely expelled more than a thousand years ago, by Islām, from its original home, where only a small remnant, some 10,000 fire-worshippers, remain, while the rest, having long ago fled from persecution to Western India, there preserve under the name of Parsis, as a prosperous community of some 100,000 souls, the religion and the learning of their ancient country. Though Zoroastrianism thus narrowly escaped being exterminated by Mohammedanism, it was in early times the religion of the great Persian Empire. From it was developed the worship of the sun-god Mithras (the Vedic Mitra). This, introduced into Rome in the first century B.C., began to be spread very widely throughout the Roman Empire, before the end of the first Christian century, by the army, the slave population, and traders, as the worship of the 'Sun-god, the unconquered Mithra' (*deus Sol invictus Mithras*). Thus by the end of the third century A.D., it bade fair to become a world-religion. At the beginning of the 4th century several Roman Emperors were votaries of Mithraism, but after the adoption of Christianity by Constantine, who became Emperor in 326 and made Christianity the official religion of the State, Mithraism declined and disappeared from Rome by the end of the 4th century.

The other three Aryan religions arose in India.

The oldest of them, Hinduism, if taken to include its earlier forms, has had a continued existence and development of more than 3,000 years in the land of its birth, where it has about 240,000,000 adherents at the present time. Jainism, its earliest offshoot, has existed in India for about 2,500 years, but is at the present day a sect with less than $1\frac{1}{2}$ million followers. A second offshoot, Buddhism, which came into being very soon after, disappeared from its native land many centuries ago, but by way of compensation spread to the north, east and south of India, to Tibet, Mongolia, China, Corea, Japan, to Burma, Siam, Indo-China, and Ceylon, becoming a world-religion of eastern Asia, with about 120,000,000 adherents.

There existed in ancient times several other forms of Aryan religion: Greek, Roman, Celtic, Teutonic, Slavonic, but all these disappeared, having been ousted in the early centuries of our era by Christianity. We possess information from their own literatures of only two of these nations, the Greeks and the Romans, while of the three others we have only Roman or Christian accounts, which, being partial or biassed, hardly supply us with adequate material for our present purpose. But of Greek religion I shall have a good deal to say, because it has so deeply influenced the civilization of the western world.

From the Semitic race issued, besides the two extinct religions the three great faiths that still survive; Judaism, Christianity, and Islām. Judaism may be considered the oldest of the ancient surviving religions, if, on the one hand, we regard its uniform character, and, on the other hand, do not include the older phases of Indo-Aryan religion in Hinduism. Its sacred book is the Old Testament written in the Hebrew language. The religion of a small people, it was expelled 1,852 years ago from its native land, Palestine, by the Romans, in consequence of the capture of Jerusalem by the Emperor Titus in the year 70 A. D. It has, during all the centuries that have elapsed since then, been preserved by the Jewish race, who number about 14,000,000, dispersed as exiles over nearly all the countries of the earth. This people has now before it the unique prospect of carrying back, in considerable numbers, its ancient religion to its original home.

While Judaism has remained a national religion with a small number of followers, its two offshoots, Islām and Christianity, have become world-religions, one having overspread the greater part of Western and Central Asia and extending across Northern Africa as far as Morocco, while the other has overflowed the whole of the continents of Europe, America, and Australia. Islām, the latest of the world-religions, was founded by Mohammed in the 7th century of our era in Arabia, its sacred book being the Quran written in Arabic, and its adherents at the present day numbering about 175,000,000.

Christianity was founded by Jesus Christ in the first century of our era in Palestine. Its sacred book is the New Testament, which is written in Greek, and its adherents number about 535,000,000. I think it will be interesting at this point to pause in order to summarize the history of the migrations and the present position of the five great religions now prevailing in the world.

1. Christianity has in the main disappeared from Asia, where it arose, but has become the religion of three other continents; it is also at the same time the religion of the western branch of the Aryans and of a progressive civilization. Thus a Semitic faith has become the religion of the western Aryans, of the white race.

2. On the other hand, an Aryan religion, Buddhism, after an existence of more than 1,000 years in its native land, India, finally disappeared from it, but having spread eastward and supplanting the primitive beliefs of those regions, became predominantly the religion of non-Aryan peoples, of the yellow race.

3. Thirdly, the Semitic religion of Arabia, while it has remained the faith of the country in which it arose, has mainly displaced the primitive religion, called Shamanism, of the greater part of another and backward division of the human race, the Turanians, whose original home was in Central Asia in the region of the Altai mountains, and who gradually occupied the central band of Asiatic territory, which extends from the confines of China to the eastern Mediterranean, as well as the north of Asia and the extreme north of Europe. The most important of the five branches of this race are the Mongols and the Turks. The latter became the most enthusiastic converts to Islām, and, as the chief propagators of that faith, have been called 'the sword of Islām.' This religion has thus become conspicuously the religion of the Turkish

peoples and the Turkish Empire. Islām also displaced the advanced Aryan religion of the Persians, as well as the Aryan faith of about one-fifth of the population of India.

4-5. The remaining two faiths, though great national religions, have never spread beyond their own countries, but have remained there from the beginning: the one, Confucianism, which is practically unchanged; the other, Hinduism, which has been modified between the period when it arose in its earliest form and the present day.

It is not difficult to explain how these two religions did not pass beyond the confines of their own countries. Confucianism is deeply rooted in specifically Chinese custom, which had already been long consolidated when that faith appeared, and which carefully avoided all contact with the outside world, as typified by the building of the Chinese wall in the second century B.C. This exclusiveness is also illustrated by an episode in the life of the famous Chinese Buddhist pilgrim Hiouen T'sang, more than 1,000 years after the death of Confucius. When early in the 7th century A.D. he started on his journey to India by way of Central Asia, he found great difficulty in escaping the vigilance of the Chinese frontier guards, and only managed to get through by stratagem, as he tells us himself in his memoirs.

The lack of a founder in Judaism and Brahmanism is due to the high antiquity of these two oldest of the surviving ancient religions. For this is characteristic of very ancient religions, which in their earliest known forms stand close to the primitive pre-historic stage, in which religion is a matter of collective or group mentality. It is only at a later stage, when individuality has been more developed, that the founder of a new religion begins his activities, having more or less the character of a reformer, impelled by the particular circumstances, political, social and religious, in which he lives, and by which the character of the new religion is determined.

Such were Zoroaster, Buddha, Confucius, Mohammed, and Christ. The four first were linked with civilizations which were of a stationary character; only the last became associated with one that was progressive, and was thus enabled to lay the foundation of the advancement of humanity more firmly than any of the others.

After this preliminary survey of the main religions of the world, I propose in the following lectures to give a brief historical as well as comparative account of each of them, with special reference to their moral side as progressing towards the service of humanity; I shall then sum up the stage at which each had or has arrived in this respect, and finally show in what points Christianity has gone beyond the rest in its progress towards the ultimate goal.

B. Primitive Religion.

As the literary records of all the religions which I am about to discuss show a comparatively advanced state of civilization among the peoples who professed them, it is advisable first to collect what is known of the earlier phase which lies behind all of them. This phase in human development is called savagery and is roughly speaking antecedent to the knowledge of writing. Without such information, the phenomena of the historical period in the sphere of morality cannot be fully understood. Much of the evidence for this remote period is supplied by what can be shown to be survivals in the historical period and by pre-historic archæology. But the most prolific source of such evidence is the science of anthropology, which furnishes us with many parallel data, virtually equivalent to contemporary evidence, from the life of the many races that have remained savages down to the present day, such as the Veddas of Ceylon, the Todas of the Nilgiris, the Andaman Islanders, the Natives of Australia, all of whom are at the lowest end of the scale, besides others who are more advanced, such as the Red Indians of America and various tribes of the Turanians. Even here we are not at the beginning of moral evolution, for we find that savage conduct already rests on a moral or semi-moral basis. Of the still more remote phase of human development to which this points, we know nothing and can only form conjectures.

The essential features of the savage phase of society from which the civilized stage was evolved, are these. Generally speaking, custom is the only bond that unites savage society; here habit prevails as resting on an only sub-conscious moral standard. The life of savages is that of a herd: their association is so close and constant that it prevents the development of personality and independent character. The normal individual here has no chance of secluding himself: hence he cannot reflect, but only imitates his neighbours. You might suppose that no progress could ever be made in such an atmosphere of mutual imitation. It is, however, made, somewhat in the same way in which fashions of dress change in civilized society. A leading anthropologist (Spencer-Gillen) says, for instance, that the Australian native is bound hand and foot by custom, but he at the same time points out that according to native traditions, far-reaching alterations, for example in the marriage system, have occasionally been brought about by powerful individuals among the people. At a rather higher level of savage society, there was a famous head-chief of the Zulus named Chaka, who showed himself to be a conscious and far-seeing innovator. But in spite of occasional incipient individuality, it may be said that the savage is a blind conservative, content to follow the customs of his forefathers. A want of moral freedom results; for the moral sanction of savages comes from without, not from within. Their conduct is governed by what is known as the "psychology of the crowd"; but there is this difference: while the civilized crowd is only a temporary gathering, the savage community is a permanent and organic association of this type. Here each man looks outwards, receiving his impulse from his neighbours in the mass, or at most from the slightly more self-determined ring-leader: a judgment resulting in approbation or disapproval is formed, or a course of action is taken, like that of a flock of sheep hurrying through a gap with one sheep at their head. The conduct of the savage is thus the result of an impression existing in, and proceeding from, the social group to which the individual belongs. It is in fact the consequence of customary morality: custom here meaning the sum of the forces of social suggestion that operate at any time in a given community.

The difficulty in savage life of maintaining communications renders it necessary to keep together in a crowd. The eminent Danish anthropologist Westermarck is doubtless quite right in making local contiguity the all-important bond of primitive life, more cogent even than kinship. The surroundings of the savage consist of several circles; but the true centre of moral influence for him is that inner circle within which he finds the most intimate and permanent association. For one type of community this social focus will be the family, for another the kin-group, for another the village. But whatever to the savage corresponded most closely to our 'home,' it was there that charity began, and indeed ended. Thus whatever may have been the case in the remotest period of human development, we must bear in mind that the savage as known to us has always looked upon himself as a member of a social group, individualism being a product of civilization. Further, the actual way in which the savage finds the members of his society grouped together, suggests the notion of how all the things of the universe are grouped together. Thus in his mind the whole universe is socialized and anthropomorphized. Lacking our mechanical control over nature, the savage has little or nothing but his moral standard to serve as his guide (his *niti* as it might be called in

Sanskrit) in dealing with friend or foe. So far is he from being unmoral, that morality may truly be said to be his all in all. His morality has of course not been thought out; but by it alone he feels his way through all his relations with his human neighbours and with the surrounding universe which for him is only human society on an enlarged scale. There are three main elements by which the conduct of savages is determined, two physical: heredity and environment; and one moral: social tradition. I need here deal with the last only.

Social tradition is enforced chiefly by religion. The function of the latter here is to inculcate the good by making anything sacred through the feeling of awe. Amongst savages, the notion of *tabu* (a Polynesian word used by anthropologists, roughly corresponding to the Latin *sacer*, from which comes the English 'sacred') is applied to all sorts of things—living beings, plants, material objects, ceremonies, words, places, times—which have the common quality of being mystically dangerous as not to be lightly approached. The reason for this is that they are considered *māna* (another Polynesian word used by anthropologists), meaning 'mystically powerful.' Now to be dangerous, because powerful, in a mystic (that is, mysterious or supernatural) way, is a quality that may be connected with bad things as well as good. Hence religion, which is concerned with the mystically good, has at first much in common with magic, which only in the long run is separated from religion, to become a synonym for all 'dealings with the devil,' that is, for all use of mystically impressive means of effecting bad and anti-social ends. It is for this reason that the *Atharvaveda*, the contents of which are largely magical, for a long time failed to attain canonical recognition in Brahmanism. Thus religion consecrates the good, as far as it is embodied in the rule of life handed on by each generation to the next, and by rendering it impressive helps the young generation to imitate and assimilate it. Religion in this way becomes the educator of man in morality.

If we wish to estimate the religious and moral standard reached by savages, it will, I think, be advisable to classify the various manifestations of their conduct and mentality under two general heads: (1) their transcendental relations, *i. e.*, their attitude towards the supernatural powers, their religious beliefs and practices; (2) their human relations, *i.e.*, their morality. The moral relation of the savage to other human beings falls into three groups: inasmuch as he is (*a*) the centre of a home circle as the social focus; (*b*) the centre of a political circle; (*c*) a member of the human race, when he is brought into touch with men belonging to some political body other than his own. But his human or moral relations extend inwards as well as outwards, in other words, he has a duty to himself, being committed to certain types of conduct that are primarily self-regarding, though they are never exclusively so, any more than his conduct towards his neighbour can ever be exclusively other-regarding or altruistic. There is thus a fourth aspect of primitive man's moral actions, those relating to himself. His ethical actions may accordingly be classified under two main heads, the second having four sub-divisions.

When I come to treat the various ancient religions later on, I propose to follow this same classification, because it is applicable to the development of mankind throughout its whole course as known to history, in its civilized as well as its savage phases. In fact these two phases are essentially similar, in spite of appearances to the contrary. Civilized man differs radically but little from savage man. The general direction of the search for the good has not altered much. The best proof of this is, that education, *i. e.*, the mere substitution of one social tradition for another, can do wonders for the born savage; again, a whole race may shake off the slumber of centuries, as the Japanese have done, and enrol themselves among the more civilized nations. On the other hand, the experience of the late world-war has shown how a nation that has reached a very high degree of intellectual culture may suddenly sink in moral conduct to the level of savages. It is probably correct to say that human nature, having a bias towards virtue, needs only the removal of its ignorance of means by which virtue is acquired, to rise to a higher level of morality. Again, the nature of primitive man has been misjudged and described as unmoral owing to inadequate study or insufficient opportunities of observation on the part of early explorers and missionaries. Thus the morality of the Australian aborigines was formerly described as having absolutely no virtues. But the more recent researches of trained anthropologists have shown that this estimate is by no means true. It is now recognised that morality is not to be judged by relationship to some fixed absolute standard, but is fundamentally related to the system of social control prevailing within the group in question. It must be remembered that the 'higher race' in its first contact seldom sees the lower at its best. Thus the ignorance and brutality of many of the first white settlers and explorers of Australia constantly provoked the natives to retaliate. The qualities of the latter were often misinterpreted. Thus they were considered to be unspeakably lazy; but this opinion was largely due to the fact that they did not show much inclination to work hard in the interests of foreign settlers. On the other hand, they displayed the most surprising industry in the collection of food and in the preparation for, and performance of, their elaborate ceremonials. There is testimony to the fact that the Australian native is possessed in a marked degree of fortitude in the endurance of suffering, this quality of mind being particularly developed in the painful ordeals of initiation.

LECTURE II

PRIMITIVE RELIGION (*concluded*).

Let us now examine the religious and ethical standard of savage society.

What was the savage's attitude to the supernatural powers? There can be no doubt that primitive man originally regarded as good only what tended to preserve the life and promote the welfare of himself and his kin. But the good soon began to be moralized, and it is a mistake to think that the savage is capable of imagining a material good only. It is true, however, that his religion as a whole amounts to this formula, half a spell and half a prayer: 'May I receive blessings and be exempt from evils.' The manner in which he thinks he can secure these results is closely bound up with his conception of the universe. Nature and matter in the modern sense have at most a very limited meaning to the typical savage. He regards his environment as a series of personal or semi-personal beings, all mystically powerful, and as such able to benefit or injure him and his. His universe is thus a moral order with which he desires to be in sympathetic social relations. He cannot imagine any part of creation that is purely unmoral and mechanical in its mode of operation. He is therefore too ready to deal with physical necessities, not like modern civilized man, by the conquest of nature, but by means of the moral suasion and control with which his mixture of religion and magic supplies him. He believes he can set in motion by propitiation or mechanical coercion the various phenomena and objects of nature as having a will-power like that of man himself, and capable of being good as a friend and evil as an enemy. Such a belief clothes itself in many forms, as the belief in a supreme being who makes the tribal laws, or again in the cult of the dead and especially of ancestral heroes : all these beliefs evidently lead in the direction of righteousness.

While the religious beliefs vary infinitely among savages, their ceremonial customs, which are far more closely and directly related to the practice of these religions, have much that is common to all. Thus *tabu*, starting from the avoidance of sacred things, becomes almost universally moralized as a purity of heart, which strengthened by a custom of ceremonial purification, develops into the confession of sins. Communion, again, is at its lower end, little more than the crudest form of sympathetic magic ; nevertheless at the upper end of the scale of evolution, it expresses the realization of the good perhaps better than any other idea within the range of religion or philosophy. Moreover, sacrifice as a ritual act, the bestowal of a gift which the worshipper himself values, passes insensibly into self-sacrifice. Thus the natural feelings and conceptions of early man in his savage state, who cannot, so to speak, see beyond the circle of his own camp, contain the germ of ideas that can unify mankind and lead it towards the ultimate goal of the service of humanity.

Of what kind is the conduct of the savage towards his fellow men ? Here we have first to consider 4 the domestic group. It is surprising to find that in this sphere the institution of marriage is universal, even among those savages who in nearly every respect have the most rudimentary culture of all, such as the Andaman Islanders, the Veddas, and the Bushmen. By marriage I mean not a loose bond, but a fixed relationship which has been defined as an exclusive relation of one or more men to one or more women, based on custom and supported by public opinion and, where law exists, by law. We thus find that among savages 'the basis of society is the family,' as the eminent anthropologist Edward Tylor has said, corroborating the statement made by the great Greek philosopher Aristotle more than 2,200 years ago. In the home circle, the 'social focus' of the savage, where the virtues connected with social intercourse are fostered by mutual relations of special intimacy, these relations may be considered under two heads: (*a*) those between the sexes, in particular between husband and wife; (*b*) those between old and young, in particular between parents and children.

(*a*) The adult savage woman is normally a wife and mother, and it is in this capacity that she is primarily related to the community regarded as a moral whole. Her function is that of directly propagating and nourishing the race, while the function of the male is protective, *i.e.*, that of indirectly preserving the race. It is probable that in a normal savage community both sexes are happy, as there are no unmarried females free or anxious to have a hand in the work of the males. Physically the woman's is perhaps the harder lot. It is a great gain to her when life becomes comparatively sedentary. For amongst hunting peoples she must not only carry her infant, but she must necessarily be the carrier in general, that the men may be free to use their weapons. Sexual life begins early, *i.e.*, as soon as puberty is reached, sometimes even before. Thus the savage female is apt to grow old more rapidly than the male. On the other hand, the male is much more liable to be cut off in the prime of life.

Not only is genuine marriage characteristic of savage society, but also an institution connected with it which, more than any other, decides the relative status of male and female, and in particular of husband and wife. This is the custom of exogamy or marrying outside the kin-group, but inside the wider circle of the tribe. This practice survives in a modified form in India, being a feature of the caste system, where the *gotra* represents the kin-group and the caste takes the place of the tribe. A few of the lowest peoples, mostly degenerate remnants, are without this practice, but it is typical of primitive society as a whole. The origin of the custom of exogamy is quite obscure; for as it meets us in history, it is a fully developed institution, both legal and religious as regards its sanctions Another general element in the social tradition of savages is one that bears strongly and on the whole very hardly on the moral status of the woman and the wife. This is the magico-religious notion that woman, and specially woman's blood, is sacred. It has various harmful results on the life of women. One of them is the long and weakening confinements they undergo at different periods of their lives (at puberty, during pregnancy, and at childbirth). Another is the avoidance on the part of the male, of what a woman has touched, for fear the contagion of effeminacy should be incurred. On the other hand, woman's position derives several advantages from this notion. Thus, her sacrosanctity, combined with her dependence on male protection, renders her an object of what finally developes into chivalry. For instance, among the Australians a woman acts as ambassador between warring tribes. Another result is that a strain of romantic love has been observed to be indulged in by many savages, especially warriors. Moreover, as a consequence of various *talus* on sexual intercourse observed by the hunter, the warrior, and the medicine man, sexual purity develops into a virtue which is of far-reaching influence on the character, as in the case of the *Brahmacā ī* in the Brahmanic system of the four orders of life among the twice-born castes in India. Savages loathe and abominate what they regard as sexual impurity when it takes the form of incest, which means death to the guilty parties.

Owing to their mystical quality women sometimes become leaders of society. As a sex they sometimes come to dominate a whole department of social activity. Thus the women of the Iroquois tribe of American Indians controlled agriculture, because they possessed a special knowledge of it.

(*b*) As to the relations between old and young, it is to be noted in the first place that, as primitive society is normally divided into fairly definite age-grades, its customs tend to apply to these age-grades as a whole. Thus religion prescribes food *tabus* and other restrictions upon the young as a class: this incidentally teaches them to control their appetites and imposes a discipline of self-denial. The most conspicuous case of all is, that the young are subjected as a class to initiation, and their moral education is administered by the society as a whole in a form that is made impressive by solemn rites associated with the infliction of considerable pain. This custom of initiation has survived in India in the form of the *upanayana* of the twice-born castes.

As regards the relation between parents and children, the education supplied by the former tends among savages to be mild. Corporal punishment is sparingly applied, chiefly because of natural affection, but sometimes, as among the Indians of North America, on the principle that a future warrior should not tolerate a blow from anyone. The mother looks after the daughter till she marries, imparting to her the duties and technical skill of women. The son, on the other hand, is often taken away from the mother and sisters some time before puberty, and made to join the company of males who tend to live more or less segregated from the females in club-houses. Education, as imparted by either parent in the case of both boys and girls, is a mixture of technical and moral instruction.

To children much affection is usually shown in spite of the fact that infanticide is practised among many of them. On the other hand, the old and infirm are treated with less solicitude by the young and are often killed off. These practices, which appear cruel according to our standard, should not be judged too severely from the point of view of the easier circumstances of civilized life. They are the direct result of pressing economic conditions, where a useless mouth, or a drag on the mobility of the group, is a handicap in the struggle for existence too heavy to be borne. They are often very much mitigated. Thus Spencer-Gillen states that certain Australian tribes rarely practised infanticide except immediately after birth, and then only when the mother thought she was unable to care for the babe. The killing of the new-born child was thus an effort of kindness : it was certainly not cruel in the eyes of the perpetrators, since they believed that the spirit-part went back to the spot whence it came, and was subsequently born to the same woman. Sometimes after the family amounted to three or four, all additional children were killed, because they would make more work than the woman could manage. In one tribe infanticide unquestionably arose through the difficulty of carrying a baby, when there were other young children, some of whom might be unable to walk. Under these circumstances, new-born infants were simply left behind when the family were on the march, for it was not regarded as killing to dispose of them in this way.

As to the old and infirm, their treatment at least among the Australian savages, was, according to the account of most observers, quite humane. The typical savage, moreover, regards his elders, alive or dead, as the embodiment of wisdom and power, with something of the supernatural in it. Ancestor worship, a special type of cult emerging from funeral rites, which universally show awe and respect rather than mere fear of the dead, and especially of one's own dead, is but the consummation of a natural sentiment which associates the imitation of their elders by the young with a sort of love that develops into filial piety and gratitude. Here you find the roots of ancestor worship which as you will see is found in so many religions.

2. Beside the strictly family group, we find in savage

society the kin-group, according to which the child belongs either to his mother's or his father's kin, and as such shares in a moral system of rights and duties from which one or other parent is cut off by *tabus* as by a wall; and in case of a conflict between groups, parent and child may find themselves actually ranged against each other. On the other hand, as far as it extends the consciousness of kin is a moral factor of the highest importance. For it involves the principle of corporate responsibility manifested in blood-revenge and similar developments of private law; while in a religious way it implies the sense of a mystic brotherhood.

3. We now come to the third and still wider group of moral relations, that which is the sphere of political virtues. Here the moral bond uniting those who are, by reason of local contiguity, in constant touch with each other, is narrow, because the area is necessarily a limited one. What corresponds with the savage to the sentiment and idea of the body politic is an aggregate of which he feels himself to be an actual part, not merely symbolically a unit: a crowd in which he is lost, in the life and movement of which his whole being is absorbed. As the hard life of such a society eliminates the coward and the loafer, the savage will normally answer to a call of duty in its sterner forms, as when public danger threatens. Nowhere is this more manifest than at the higher level of savagery at which the 'king' appears, as the living personification of the body politic. Loyalty at this point becomes almost identical with patriotism, and it is absolute. Thus the Fijian criminal stands, unbound, to be killed: for he says: 'whatever the king says must be done'; and the native of Dahomey exclaims: 'my head belongs to the king; if he wishes to take it, I am ready to give it up.'

The kindlier side of political duty, as manifested in friendliness and good fellowship, is conspicuous in unspoilt savages, their dances, games, festivals, and perpetual gatherings being possible solely on that condition. Under their traditional system the Australian natives lived a harmonious and certainly far from unhappy life. One observer says they were a merry race. A certain tribe was noted to have lived most peaceably; for instance, a camp of 300 is known to have continued for three months without a quarrel.

As among the lower savages a primitive form of communism or socialism tends to prevail, the scope for generosity is narrow; so is that of honesty, for both these virtues can only be developed in an individualistic system. Thus stealing is not a crime within the home circle, though in the wider circle of the tribe it may lead to friction between groups. On the other hand, as practised against those who are outside this circle, *i.e.*, against strangers and enemies, it is rather a virtue, at least amongst peoples of a predatory type. A survival of this moral attitude is probably to be found in the practice of the thieves' caste in southern India. It also survived in the cattle-raiding habits which still prevailed in the Highlands of Scotland hardly two centuries ago. Veracity is at this primitive stage more or less on the same level as honesty: intimates and comrades do not deceive each other, but to lie to outsiders is regarded as diplomatic. This view seems not altogether to have died out even at the present day in the international relations of civilized peoples.

There are three phenomena of savage man's relation to his neighbour, which I must not pass over. One of them is a social institution which though unknown at the level of the lower savagery, is wide-spread at a higher level: the institution of slavery. This introduces into savage society a class of persons without legal rights, who may indeed be war-captives or a subject race dominated by invaders, but may also be broken men and pawns of the same flesh and blood as their owners. It seems, however, that the slave is treated more humanely in a savage society than he would be if exploited in the interests of a developed industrialism. But life, when it is not that of the nearest and dearest, is cheap among savages: and the constant association of a slave-owning system with bloody rites involving human sacrifice, as in West Africa, shows how much inhumanity it must produce. Moreover, wherever a slave-trade is established, the horrors involved in it are bound to have a demoralizing effect. Africa is the standing instance of a continent rotted to the core by such an institution. It is melancholy to think that civilization is most to blame for its development. Another melancholy thought is this: slavery though morally an abomination, is nevertheless possibly one of the main causes of human evolution. War brought slavery; slavery promotes agriculture; agriculture of all things favours and establishes settled institutions and peace, as the late Professor Tylor, the anthropologist, has observed.

4. As regards international morality, it finds but little scope in savage society, because morality at this stage of development is primarily an affair of the home-circle. Within this, amity of a highly emotional quality prevails, outside of it, enmity fierce and uncompromising. But beyond the home-circle there are inter-gentile relations with a wider group that savagery respects. These pass almost imperceptibly into inter-tribal relations (which may here be called international relations). Thus in Australia the kin-groups and the local groups are loosely combined into tribes, and these again in wider combinations known to ethnologists as 'nations.' The relations between the lesser and the wider groups spread so far that a native can, it appears, travel almost from one end of Australia to another without being treated as a complete stranger. Possibly the stranger as such here tends, as among other savages, to be sacred, hospitality thus having a religious sanction, since the fear of a stranger's curse, as Westermarck has shown, proves a not ineffective substitute for the stimulus of generosity. In Australia there are thus to a certain extent sympathetic relations, owing to the race and culture

being largely uniform, between groups more widely separated than can be the case where the difference in these two respects is greater.

It is not till a fuller control over the forces of nature than primitive man possessed, enables a population to grow relatively dense, that the struggle for room begins in a given area, and the predatory spirit is let loose. This is, in fact, the economic cause that has started world migrations, such as notably that of the nomad Turanian race from east to west, which has had so momentous an effect on the history of the world. The earliest historical evidence of this particular movement is to be found in the Avestic references to the conflicts between the nomad Turkic people and the settled agricultural Aryans of Persia. Under these economic conditions war begins to be evolved, and the art of killing one's neighbour efficiently and systematically no doubt took some time to develop. It was not fully developed till within the last ten years. In protected areas a mild type of savage flourishes, to whom war is unknown. Thus the Todas of the Nilgiris have literally no man-killing weapons at all. The fighting qualities would appear to go closely with the breed, and to be intensified by conflict with dangerous man-slaying animals, which *e.g.*, are not to be found on the Australian continent. The accompaniments of primitive warfare are mainly what have given savagery its evil name, being precisely that aspect of the life of savage society which is turned, not without good reason, towards the so-called pioneers of civilization. But as regards themselves, war is often a transitory condition, though there are some definitely predatory peoples, such as the Zulus and the Masai of Africa, and some tribes of North America. The characteristic quality of the savage brave is fierceness, an emotional rather than a calm and reasoned form of valour. As such it sustains itself partly by war dances before the event, but partly also by wanton cruelty both during battle and afterwards in the torturing of prisoners, as among the American Indians, who thereby not only satisfied their feelings, but also kept up a standard of frightfulness in the future warriors of their tribe.

One form of the revolting practice of cannibalism is directly associated with warfare; that is, a warrior tribe will eat its enemies simply as it were to glut its rage. There can, moreover, be little doubt that the institution amounts to an asset in the struggle for existence, as cannibalism inspires terror amongst the neighbouring peoples, so that a cannibal tribe, like the Niam-Niam in Africa, may rank amongst the most vigorous and effective people of a given region. What the origin of this loathsome institution was, it is impossible to say. It may have been the result of war; thus the Niam-Niam and the Monbuttu tribes carry on wars for the sake of obtaining human flesh, as if they were a kind of hunting expedition. The eating of both friends and foes slain in battle has a magical notion as its basis; for savages eagerly desire certain kinds of food in order that they may acquire the mental or bodily qualities of the man or animal from which the meat is derived: thus the heart of a lion is recommended for a warrior to make him brave. The origin of Mexican cannibalism can be traced to the widespread custom of eating food offered to the gods. The Aztec worship of the god of war led to the sacrifice of prisoners, and the custom of sacrifice led to their frequent wars. Another form of cannibalism is the practice of devouring dead kinsmen, as the most respectful method of disposing of their remains. The object here was to keep the spirit in the family; and this is not without high moral value, though connected with so revolting a custom. Most kinds of cannibalism came to be surrounded with religious ceremonial.

The custom of cannibalism still prevails or prevailed until recently in many parts of the world, in West and Central Africa, New Guinea, Melanesia (especially Fiji) and Australia, in various East Indian islands, and in South America. The evidence of palæolithic cave-dwellings in France show that it was at least occasionally practised in Europe in prehistoric times. And there can be no doubt that cannibalism was once a world-wide practice among savages. But whatever moral effect the form of cannibalism connected with war may have had on savages, that of war itself both on the group and the individual probably made as much for good as for evil. Collectively men are here knit together by a common purpose that demands from them at once all the 'preliminary virtues' as Bagehot calls them: courage, loyalty, obedience, and a devotion maintained to the point of death. For the individual again, war is a school for self-respect; and though the swagger and boasting of the savage brave has its humourous aspect, his mastery over that lower self which urges him to shun danger and to live a soft life, is reflected in a strength of character (*dhairya* in Sanskrit) to which is added, on the intellectual and ideal side, a sense of honour and of duty. This sentiment has probably counted for more in the history of the race than even the religious sense of *tabu*, inasmuch as the defiance of a danger that is known is more rational than the avoidance of a danger that is unknown and is only taken to be a danger because it is unknown.

5. We have still to consider the self-regarding morality of the savage. It is precisely here that the morality of the savage is especially weak. This is due to the fact that he looks outward, not inwards, and reads his duty in the movements of his fellows, not in the movements of his own heart. He has his selfish inclinations which have to be suppressed by social drill and education; but he has little of that moral individuality which enables a man to stand out for the right, even against the opinion of his circle. He sees as one of the crowd, and at most applies his crowd-consciousness to himself as to one who is viewed from without. It may be said that his most internal moral sanction is pride of appearance. He therefore shows a tendency to self-adornment,

which unfortunately is not always accompanied by the virtue of personal cleanliness. The savage also shows a desire to cultivate an honourable idleness: to abstain from such work as may lower his dignity. This is directly due to pride of self. In fact the savage is something of a gentleman, and has in some cases been described as the 'noble savage' It is from being unable to appreciate this aspect of him that the civilized man has not generally established satisfactory relations with the savage. On the higher side, the pride of the savage gives him an intense sense of his rights and especially of his right to a good name: so that he must not tolerate an insult to himself or to those who are intimately connected with him. Moreover, the curious power that man alone among animals has of putting an end to his own life is the occasion among some savages of exalting suicide to a place among the virtues because it is an opportunity of dying with dignity as the counterpart of living with dignity.

In closing the subject of primitive religion, I may say that there is no country in the world in which the study of anthropology can be so fruitfully pursued or in which such study would do more for the furtherance of enlightenment.

Selected Bibliography

Tylor, *Anthropology*, 1881; *Primitive Culture*, 1891. A. Lang, *Myth, Ritual and Religion*, 1887. Ratzel, *History of Mankind* (Eng. Tr.), London, 1896-8. Sutherland, *The Origin and Growth of the Moral Instinct*, 1896. Frazer, *The Golden Bough*, 1900. Westermarck, *Origin and Development of the Moral Ideas*, London, 1906-8. L. T. Hobhouse, *Morals in Evolution*, London, 1906. W. McDougall, *An Introduction to Social Psychology*, London, 1908. R. R. Marett, *Anthropology*, 1912.

A. The Religion of China.

We now come to the historical stage of religion and morality, the earliest phases of which we find recorded for the most part in the sacred books of the ancient religions.

I propose to examine first the system of the Chinese, who possess the oldest surviving civilization in the world. The Chinese race presents a remarkable contrast in many essential respects to the Indian branch of the Aryan stock. The Chinese are preëminently a practical race; the Indians a spiritual and an idealistic one. The Chinese have always shown a strong taste for recording historical facts, having chronicles for every year going back many centuries before the Christian era; the Indians have no works of a historical character till long after 1000 A. D. The Chinese evolved their own indigenous system of writing in remote antiquity; the Indians like the Greeks, borrowed their alphabet from a foreign race, the Phœnicians, at a comparatively late date, probably not earlier than 700 B. C. The Chinese have directed their intellectual interest to morality, the Indians theirs to religion and philosophy. Both, however, have the point in common that their ancient civilizations were arrested in their development and became more or less stationary at much about the same period, the Indians having been dominated ever since by the doctrines of *karma* and transmigration and the social organization of caste; the Chinese by a system of ethics which has permeated their whole national life.

One sometimes hears the remark that all religions are practically the same. The following lectures will I think show that this is a misleading statement. It is true that nearly all the main religions have the same goal before them: the realization of the good or salvation; and a few of them have independently arrived at some important doctrines in which they agree. But each of them represents a different stage in various aspects. In some, the conception of god is more spiritual than in others. Some are polytheistic, others are purely monotheistic. Several are idolatrous, others are not. The standard of morality which they sanction is also different: thus some sanction polygamy, others insist on monogamy. Lastly, in the relation of man to his neighbour, some religions do not go beyond the national standpoint, others are more universal.

The Chinese system means the morality of the school of Confucius only, for there is no other system in China. The Confucian moral principles and rules are those pervading the Chinese classical literature, which for 2,500 years has been studied by every scholar throughout the length and breadth of China. This body of morals has been accepted without question by all Chinese whether educated or not; it has moulded the social life of the people and has pervaded the administration and legislation of the nation. Taoism and Buddhism, it is true, have taken their place beside Confucianism as religions, because they satisfy better the cravings of the human heart with regard to a future life, but their morality is borrowed from Confucianism. In Confucianism pure and simple, there is practically nothing of a religious nature. It adopts an attitude of reserve on questions relating to the unseen world; it is silent regarding sin and its remedy; and its references to the possibility and value of prayer are equivocal.

It must not be supposed that the moral system of Confucius destroyed the previous indigenous religion of China. By no means. That religion has survived in and beside Confucianism down to the present day.

Though Confucius has given his name to a school, he did not claim to have founded one. He said of himself that he was a transmitter, not a creator, believing in and loving the ancients. His name is known to us in the Latinized form of the Chinese *Kung fu tze*, the philosopher king. His system is known in China as the 'School of the Learned' or 'of

Scholars.' This represents orthodoxy in China, all other systems being heterodox, though Taoism and Buddhism have as a result of long association been popularly admitted to a place among the 'three schools.' Taoism is based on the same ancient material as that on which Confucius drew. Lao-tze, to whom is attributed the system known as Tao-kiao, or 'School of the Way,' commonly called Taoism (from Tao 'way'), was a strenuous reformer who boldly applied the teachings which he found in the ancient Chinese records to the improvement of existing conditions, making non-interference and the suppression of personal ambition the keystones of his system. Buddhism, on the other hand, was an exotic, which making its way into China by way of Central Asia from India, easily found in its Mahāyāna form a footing there, as it supplied a want in Confucianism, with its doctrines of an All-merciful One, its spiritual aids and consolations, its plans of salvation, and its theory of a 'Western Paradise.'

Confucius was born, when the Chow dynasty established in 1122 B. C. was on the decline, in the year 551 B. C. and died in 478 B. C. He was thus an almost exact contemporary of Buddha, the date of whose death has been calculated with great probability to have taken place about 480 B. C. It is most remarkable that these two great reformers should have founded at the same time, but in different countries lying so far apart, two systems which agree in being characteristically moral rather than religious, and in which one of the greatest doctrines of moral conduct known in the history of civilization was simultaneously enunciated, a doctrine which also agrees with one of the fundamental teachings of Christianity.

From 530 B.C. onwards Confucius devoted himself for thirty years to the work of teaching, and gradually collected around him an enthusiastic band of disciples, while the last five years of his life he gave up to the completion of his literary labours connected with the ancient records, and to the production of his one original work, the "Spring and Autumn Annals." In order to understand the moral system of Confucius thoroughly, it must be borne in mind that he was above all things a political reformer, who based his political principles on a moral foundation. He was born in a period of political unrest, and the great object towards which he directed his activities was the tranquillization of the Chinese empire. The possibility of accomplishing this aim he endeavoured to realize in three ways. In the first place, by his editions of the ancient historical records and poetry, he aimed at showing to his own and to all future ages the method by which the great rulers of antiquity had succeeded in controlling and directing their subjects. A second means consisted in personal instructions and counsels to the various rulers of numerous feudal states, to journeys through which he devoted some thirteen years of his life (496-483), and in teaching the ardent students who delighted to gather around him.

The cardinal view which he so often emphasized was that if sage and sovereign could be combined in one person, the difficulties of ruling the empire would disappear. The force of example was the great motive power he sought to apply everywhere in morals: if the lord paramount would only imitate the ancient worthies, the various princes would be excited to emulation, and thus through every grade of society the process would be continued until the whole nation was reformed. Confucius thus concentrated his efforts on the education of rulers, believing that if he should succeed in implanting his opinions amongst the higher classes, the regeneration of the masses would follow as a matter of course. As aids to effecting his purpose Confucius could only propose the illustrious examples of antiquity which he delighted in discovering and popularizing. He could promise no assistance from religion, or, as it is expressed in Chinese, from Heaven; for man must depend on his own unaided abilities, upon his nature which he had received from Heaven. For the

Confucian gospel is based upon the conviction that man's nature is originally good, and merely requires cultivation on right lines to bring it to its highest perfection. Man's nature being predisposed towards goodness, he must allow its full development in harmony with the observed course of nature, and the examples of the great sages of the past. Confucius wished the world of men to reflect the harmony of nature. Hence the very first essential in his system was the cultivation of knowledge, especially natural science. The steps in the process of self-culture were these. The completion of knowledge leads to sincerity in thought, for the reason that the scholar who has thus attained enlightenment can no longer be deceived by outward appearance or inward imaginings. Bieng thus freed from the deceptive influence of passion, emotion, fear, and so forth, he is able to rectify his heart, that is, to restrain wayward thoughts, feelings, and tendencies, in other words to practise self-restraint. His outward actions then come to conform to the highest ideals of propriety: from now he becomes a centre of influence extending to his family and his state, so that by such self-cultivation, when generally practised, the whole empire is made tranquil and happy. Since, according to Confucius, men are by nature nearly alike, becoming widely different by practice only, what is prescribed for rulers should, to a certain extent, apply to the mass of the people also: though they may not be able to pursue their studies to the same degree, all must share in the process of self-culture and thus bear a part in the tranquillization of the Empire. Confucius admitted that the gifts of nature varied greatly, but in spite of their diversities it was possible for a man by means of self-culture to reach the highest development of which his nature is capable, and nothing less than this should satisfy him. 'Rest in the highest,' or 'cease only when the acme is reached,' is the key-note of the 'Great Learning,' an extremely short treatise on the practice of virtue and the art of governing, which is perhaps admired by the Chinese beyond all their other canonical books. Though perhaps not written by Confucius himself, it substantially agrees with his views and must have been written not long after his time.

After thus stating briefly the circumstances of the times in China when Confucius appeared on the stage, and his general method of dealing with them, we may now turn to considering his system in some detail. You remember that in describing the ethics of primitive man I divided the whole field into five parts. It will, I think, conduce to clearness if I follow the same plan in discussing Confucianism.

With regard to religion, Confucius certainly countenanced the observances of his time in so far as they were in consonance with ancient custom ; but he did not openly attack the religious abuses, extravagances, and decadence which prevailed, but only sought to restrain popular superstitions. Otherwise he adopted an attitude of strict reticence towards the question of religion, deprecating a too close inquiry into spiritual phenomena. He added nothing to the contemporary knowledge of god or of spirits ; he had nothing to say about death or the hereafter, the present being the sole stage on which he sought to inspire men to act their part. In the only book which he himself composed, the 'Spring and Autumn' annals of his native state, there are no references to religious observances ; and in the conversations recorded by his disciples, the name of Shang-ti is only once mentioned, and the discussion of transcendental subjects is distinctly deprecated. Confucius always refused to talk of supernatural phenomena or of supernatural beings.

The worship of ancestors, which had come down from ancient times, was, as practised by Confucius, merely a commemorative rite. There is no sanction from his authority for its more objectionable features in later times in China : the transformation of the dead into tutelary deities and the absurd doctrine that the fortunes of a family are determined by the location of its tombs. Perhaps Confucius was inclined to overlook the extravagant attention paid to ancestor worship because it served to emphasize his own doctrines of divine right (the Emperor is a son of Heaven), and the supreme importance of acquiescence in the prevailing political order. He anticipated St. Paul in saying "Let every soul be in subjection to the higher powers; the powers that be are ordained by God." The appointment of a new ruler is described as the receiving of Heaven's decree : every subject of the state must therefore fulfil his part with unconditional loyalty to the head of the state.

Though it was as a teacher of practical morality that Confucius became famous, he left no treatise on the subject, nor did he ever handle it systematically. We have from him merely a quantity of disconnected utterances which were collected and recorded by his followers, or appear as quotations in later writers.

In the Confucian system there are five cardinal relations on which the whole social structure is based : those which exist between father and son, elder brother and younger brother, husband and wife, friend and friend, sovereign and subject. The duties implied in the first three belong to the circle of the family, which in this system is emphatically the basis of society. Filial piety is the most important domestic duty of the Chinese. Similar to it, but less important, is fraternal affection, or the duty which a younger brother owes to an elder. These two duties formed the corner-stone of both the ethical and the social system of Confucius. For upon them depend not only the self-culture of the individual, but also the regulation of the family and the government of the state. It is by practising them that the people learn to be obedient to the government and the laws. Confucius also regarded them as the foundation of charity, the greatest of all the virtues.

Filial piety is described as consisting in serving parents when alive, burying them and sacrificing to them when dead, always in accordance with the rules of propriety. Reverence and willingness in service are requisite : mere performance of duties is not enough.

In the system of Confucius the whole field of morality is divided into five parts, each of which is the sphere of a cardinal virtue.

1. One of these, as coming within the sphere of the individual, is knowledge (including wisdom and practical sagacity). The most important kind of knowledge is the knowledge of men. A man should know the commands of Heaven, that is, what is right and what is wrong. He ought further to know the rules of propriety ; and thirdly he should know language, in order to estimate the character of those who speak with him. It is real knowledge when a man knows a thing and recognises that he knows it ; and when he does not know a thing and recognizes that he does not know it. A man should acquire knowledge for his own improvement, not in order to win approbation. But to study without thinking is labour lost ; while thought without study is dangerous. Confucius once said : 'I have passed the whole day without eating and the whole night without sleeping, occupied with thinking ; it was of no use : the better plan is to study.' The knowledge of the truth, however, is not equal to the love of it ; and the possessor of literary acquirements is a useless man, if he be void of practical ability.

2. Another of the cardinal virtues is propriety, which though a personal virtue, is an important element in a man's influence on others. It implies the idea of ceremoniousness, but does not consist in conspicuous personal adornment. It must be accompanied by reverence, but it is worthless without charity (in the sense of human kindness). Without a knowledge of propriety a man's character cannot be established, but, if combined with study, it will keep him from erring. Its absence lessens the value of other virtues : respectfulness then becomes clumsiness, carefulness becomes timidity,

boldness becomes insubordination, and straightforwardness becomes rudeness.

3. Sincerity (including good faith and truthfulness) is a virtue which seems to be of a self-regarding type, but applies only to a man's relations to others. Its necessity is inculcated in many passages of Confucian works. Truthfulness and sincerity, it is said, should be one's first principles ; without truthfulness no man can successfully make his way. In intercourse with friends it is above everything necessary to be sincere : it would be disgraceful to pretend friendship with a man whom one dislikes. Sincerity is one of the virtues required in a ruler.

4. Righteousness (including justice and duty) is the other-regarding cardinal virtue of public life. Thus to refuse to serve one's community is a failure in this virtue. The prince must be just in laying burdens on his people ; if he is so, they will willingly submit to his rule. If righteousness be absent, courage only leads men of high position into rebellion, and those of low position into brigandage. Without righteousness riches and honour are but a fleeting cloud.

5. The greatest cardinal virtue is concerned with man's relations to man, the social duty of benevolence, humanity, or charity (in St. Paul's sense of love of one's fellow men). The descriptions given by Confucius of this virtue vary according to the occasion and the questioner. The most concise is that it is 'to love all men'; the most elaborate, that it consists in 'the practice of respectfulness, indulgence, sincerity, earnestness and kindness.' On another occasion it is said to be found in reverence and the observance of the rule: 'Do not unto others what you would not wish to be done to yourself.' This great rule is repeated several times by Confucius, who once gave it as sufficient alone to serve as a guide for one's whole life. A man, he said, may be pure, loyal, capable, and yet not worthy to be called charitable. Confucius

disclaimed for himself any right to be so considered. Charity, he said, is founded on filial piety and fraternal submission ; and if rulers behave properly to their relatives, they will stimulate the people to charity. Thus we see that the golden rule that *Christ taught* was inculcated 500 years before by Confucius, that rule which has been described as the most unshaken law of morality, the foundation of all social virtue. But there is one well-known instance in which he does not go so far as the standard of benevolence preached by Christ. When asked what he thought of the repayment of injury with kindness, he replied: 'With what then will you repay kindness? Repay injury with justice, kindness with kindness.' On another occasion also, he declared in reply to an inquirer, that if his father were murdered, the son must be ready to slay the murderer whenever and wherever he should meet him.

Confucius, being a man of an eminently prosaic and practical turn of mind, was never weary of describing the characteristics of virtue, or of drawing distinctions between right and wrong in actual life; but he cared little to speculate on the nature of the moral faculty or any such questions. Nevertheless he arrived at a general view as to the nature of virtue: we know that he considered virtue to be a mean between two extremes, which some fail to reach, while others go beyond it; and he held the fault of excess to be as bad as that of defect. This doctrine agrees with that enunciated more than a century and a half later by the great Greek philosopher Aristotle, who regards virtue as a mean between excess and defect. These ideas are elaborated in the treatise called the *Doctrine of the Mean* which contains many quotations of Confucius' words, and is believed to have been written by his grandson. This treatise further declares that man receives his nature from Heaven, and when he acts in conformity with that nature, he is following the proper path, from which he must never swerve. Here we find a principle disclosed, about which Confucius never expressed himself definitely, but which for many generations occupied the minds of his followers more than any other question in ethics, namely, that the nature of all men at their birth is perfectly good. This doctrine of the goodness of human nature had its most powerful advocate in Mencius (Meng Ki, B.C. 372-289), the greatest of the learned men who followed Confucius as their master. This doctrine has found final acceptance among the Chinese. But it was not left unchallenged at first. In Mencius' own time a certain contemporary philosopher urged that man's nature is neither good nor bad, but may be led in either direction by outside influence. The theory was also urged at that time that the nature of some men is good and that of others bad. Soon after Mencius' time a distinguished scholar named Hsün Ching maintained with much force that human nature is evil, and that men are made good only by teaching and by the laws. Finally, about the time of the Christian era, the philosopher Yang Hsiung brought forward the theory that human nature is partly good and partly evil. He taught that man's progress in either direction depends on the development of the good or the bad part of his nature according as he is influenced by his environment.

It must be clear from what I have said that the Chinese had, at a comparatively early period of human development, already reached an advanced stage of moral civilization, far beyond the level attained in the pre-historical age which I previously described. We see great progress from a selfish to an altruistic, from a narrow to a wide outlook. For the very rudimentary self-regarding morality of the early stage, we have here the far-reaching principle of self-culture. The sphere of morality is no longer limited to the family circle, but starting from that circle as its basis is extended so as to include the whole nation which is now an organized empire consisting of a number of states, compared with the primitive ethnic 'nation' composed of an aggregate of tribes.

But international morality shows practically no advance. For though the comprehensive system seems to embrace the whole of humanity, and Confucius expresses the hope that the 'Middle Kingdom' will once more become a model to the barbarians on the frontiers, that part of mankind which lay beyond the confines of China remained (except, in much later times, Japan) outside its influence. Some three centuries after Confucius' death was built the great wall of China, which isolated the Empire from the outer world to a greater degree than has been the case with any other country in the whole course of history.

As we have seen, religion plays hardly any part in the Confucian system; but the latter is based, as I have already indicated, on a much more ancient system in which religion, properly so called, occupies a paramount position. There are many clear evidences in Chinese literature of the existence of religious beliefs and practices both before and after Confucius' time, and these are reflected in the imperial sacrifices offered in Peking till the end of the Empire, and still continue to be offered. The ancient religion of China, which is much older than, and continued beside and after Confucianism, is a combination of nature-worship and the worship of the dead. This nature-worship is the worship of the Universe through its parts and phenomena, a universalistic animism, a kind of polytheism, akin to that of the Vedic religion. The gods are the deities that animate heaven, the sun and moon, the stars, wind, rain, clouds, the earth, mountains, rivers, and so forth. Heaven is the chief god, who controls all spirits and their actions. No spirits can harm men without the authorization of Heaven's agents or its tacit consent. They are accordingly Heaven's agents for punishing the bad. Heaven is the highest god that exists, there being in the Chinese system no god beyond the world, no maker of it, like Yahweh, Allah, or the lower Brahmā. He is to this day called T'ien 'Heaven' or Shang-ti 'Supreme Ruler.' As the Emperor stood at the head of the whole earth, he was the head of the state religion; he acknowledged the superiority only of Heaven whose son he was. Heaven was the natural protector of his throne and house, which would inevitably perish, if by wicked conduct he forfeited Heaven's favour. The most important sacrifice offered to this god took place on the night of the winter solstice and was presented by the Emperor at Peking on the 'Altar of Heaven', which is open to the sky and is the largest altar in the world. On this altar are tablets for the spirits of the Sun, the Moon, the Great Bear, the five planets, the twenty-eight principal constellations (corresponding to the Indian *nakṣatras*), and the host of stars; also for those of the winds, clouds, rain, and thunder. Before these tablets were dishes and baskets with sacrificial articles. For all these offerings cows, goats, and swine were presented. Next to Heaven among the state divinities is Earth, whose square altar of marble, open to the sky, is situated in a vast walled park, outside Peking. Here a solemn sacrifice was offered annually by the Emperor on the day of the summer solstice to the tablet of Earth, to those of the Imperial ancestors, and to those of the chief mountains, rivers, and seas. This sacrifice continues, I understand, to be offered by the Emperor as a pensioner of the Chinese Republic.

Next in rank to Heaven and Earth in the state religion are the ancestors. Solemn sacrifices were offered to them by the Emperor in the 'Grand Temple.' These and a few others were called the 'great sacrifices.'

There are also 'middle-class sacrifices,' the state-gods worshipped in which include the Sun-god and the Moon-god, whose altars are situated outside the east and the west gate respectively of Peking; also famous men of fabulous antiquity who introduced the Tao or Order of the Universe (which in the Veda is called *ṛta*) among men, thus conferring on them the blessings of civilization, learning, and morality. These may be divided into eight groups. One of the groups here worshipped includes Confucius, together with his nearest ancestors and over seventy earlier and later exponents of his doctrine and school, all of whom have tablets in his temples throughout China. Confucius' case is a remarkable parallel to that of Buddha. Confucius would doubtless have deprecated any kind of worship of himself going beyond commemoration. Buddha objected to the worship of images, but he himself in course of time was deified and his stereotyped image has become the object of worship of more men than probably any other one in the history of the world.

As regards the method of representing deities, it is the rule to make images in human form of the gods who are believed to have lived as men, but for the others simply to put up tablets inscribed with their principal divine titles. The tablets as well as the images are supposed to be inhabited by the spirits, especially when at sacrifices these have been formally prayed to or summoned, with or without music, to descend into those objects. Confucian worship and sacrifice, thus being actually addressed to animate images, are idolatry. It is certainly quite inconsistent with the Chinese spirit to regard such tablets and images as mere painted wood.

The state religion which was administered by the son of Heaven, the Emperor, as High priest, and by ministers and mandarins throughout the empire as his proxies, is thoroughly ritualistic. An elaborate ritual, regulating in minutest detail every point was framed on the basis of the classics during the Han dynasty (beginning 200 B. C.). Since then it has been followed with modifications and additions down to the present day. The most ancient religious institutions of China can thus be studied and described in detail by Chinese scholars from official printed documents.

The state religion was instituted for the purpose of influencing the Universe by the worship of gods, in order that happiness might be secured to the Emperor, his house, and his people. It purports to ensure the good working of the Tao, or Universal order, thus frustrating the work of evil spirits. The exercise of this religion being the highest duty of rulers, the people are not allowed to take part in it, the only religion permitted to them by the State being the worship of their own ancestors, which is classical and therefore Confucian. Nevertheless the people freely indulge in the worship of Confucian deities. In villages and other localities they have temples for the worship of mountains, streams, rocks, and the like. The god of earth is in particular venerated everywhere in temples, chapels and shrines. The people also everywhere resort to state temples, and worship the idols there in their own way. As this popular worship of Confucian deities is practised all through the Empire, the images of gods exist by tens of thousands, the temples by thousands. Almost every temple has its idol gods which are co-ordinate or subordinate in rank to the chief god, so that China probably deserves to be called the most idolatrous country in the world. This religion is also practised in private houses, many of which have altars for gods and goddesses, to whom on fixed days sacrifices are annually presented.

The worship of ancestors first begins to be mentioned in 2255 B. C. It is mentioned so often in the ancient classics, and in such detail, that we cannot doubt that it was also the core of the ancient religion. It has assumed the form of a most elaborate system of disposing of the dead. Large tumuli have always been erected for princes and nobles, and magnificent mausolea built for emperors. Those of the last dynasty are among the grandest that man has ever produced.

The ancestral cult is regulated in the state ritual by special rules for all classes of the Chinese people. Many a well-to-do family possesses its ancestral temple, where the soul tablets of the older generations are preserved and where sacrifices are offered to them. In the first months and yea after the burial certain sacrifices are offered on the grav later on there is one sacrifice every year in spring.

There can be no doubt that ancestor worship has had a moralizing influence on the life of the Chinese. The punishing hand of the forefathers is always present on the house-altar and in the temple of the family, deterring many a son or daughter from evil. Ancestor worship strengthens the ties of family life, as it supplies the descendants with a rallying point in the common ancestral altar. It thus fosters a spirit of mutual help in the emergencies of life. It has undoubtedly exercised a powerful influence upon Chinese family life and social institutions.

It has, however, been made a charge against ancestor worship that it sanctions and encourages concubinage in China. This is an extremely common practice among the wealthy in China, though persons of strict morality view it with disapprobation, except where a wife is not likely to bear a son. In such a case the necessity of having male descendants to continue the ancestral sacrifices completely justifies concubinage in the opinion of all Chinese, even though it is possible to avoid the practice by the introduction into the family of an adopted child.

B. The Religion of Persia.

In Confucianism we have seen a system of morality which is almost entirely separated from religion. Let us now turn to the ancient religion of Persia, one of the branches of the Aryans, founded by Zarathuṣtra. This was and is represented by the Avesta and the Pahlavi books. Here we meet again a system of morality, but one of a totally different kind, a system of morality which is entirely bound up with and based on religion, which is in the fullest sense a religion of morality. The ancient religion of Persia is in origin more closely allied to that of the Vedas than to any other Aryan religion: but the reform of Zarathuṣtra fundamentally changed its character. Had that reform not taken place, the old Persian would have hardly differed from the old Indian religion. Even as it is, these two have a great many special points in common. But if we compare Zoroastrianism and Brahmanism generally, we find that in the former the moral interest predominates, as compared with the sacrificial and philosophical interests of the latter. This moral interest is an outcome of the practical and political character of the Persians; but its religious colouring is due to the peculiarity of the system of the *Avesta*. That system is, as you know, a dualistic one, consisting in the antagonism of two opposing spirits, the pure and good Ahura Mazda (later contracted to Ormazd by what in Sanskrit would be a Prakritization) and the impure and evil Angra Mainyu (later contracted to Ahriman). This dualism is already to be found in the *gāthās*, the oldest part of the *Avesta*, which originated perhaps in the time of the Prophet himself. It is said that when the two Spirits first met, they created as the first things Life and Death, and as the final end, Hell for the Wicked and Heaven for the righteous. Life and Death appear as two real empires, the one the dominion of Ormazd, the other that of Ahriman. The two empires not being divided into the material and the spiritual, the two powers rule together in nature, in physical as well as spiritual phenomena, as life and death, good and evil. The aim of Ormazd's empire is to further life, with a view to which his angels, the Amesha Spentas, the 'Immortal Holy Ones,' act, while the chief of the evil spirits is spoken of as 'full of death.' As moral forces the two principles may be described as Purity and Impurity, the former representing all the vital forces of the world, the latter all the forces of death. The duty of man is to uphold the forces of the good, and his moral righteousness consists in this activity. Purity, holiness, righteousness are here identical conceptions: they are all included in *aṣa*, the fundamental idea of the religion of Zoroaster, meaning 'truth' and 'right,' and corresponding exactly both phonetically and in sense (cp. the Confucian *tao*) to the Vedic *ṛta*, the 'moral law' (from the primary sense of 'natural order'). Later this sense is expressed in India by *dharma*. It is virtually identical with what is called Tao, 'the order of the Universe,' the 'right way' in China. It would be in the spirit of all three religions to say: *aṣa, ṛta, tao* is the basis of religion. Personified *aṣa* is the angel Aṣa Vahiṣta the 'best righteousness' (which in Sanskrit transliteration would be *ṛta vasiṣṭha*); this is also the name of Paradise (in modern Persian *Bahiṣt*).

This conception of righteousness represents what is the final aim of religion: the regeneration of the world, the realization of the good, the removal of all the impurity of evil and death.

The dualistic doctrine of the Avestic *gāthās* is represented in a mythological form in the Pahlavi book called *Būndahish* The evil spirit is here represented as endeavouring to destroy what the good spirit created. Though he is overcome, his evil work is allowed to be continued in the world for a period. The purpose of this is to make clear how bad the evil is, and as a contrast to inculcate that good deeds and a good life represent the only right in the world. This period is to last for 6,000 years, the duration of the actual world, after the expiry of which the processes of the final victory of Ormazd begin. The world-period is thus a time of struggle between the powers of good and evil. The later *Avesta* (called *Vendīdād*) represents the beginning of the conflict as a twofold creation, in which Ahriman always creates something evil to counterbalance every good thing created by Ormazd. In this way nature becomes twofold, good things and creatures always mingling with the evil and wicked.

The world of spirits is divided into good and evil, as well as the world of men: Ahriman being the chief not only of evil spirits, but of human unbelievers as well. The great problem of life is: shall Ormazd or Ahriman prevail, and how is the cause of Ormazd to be furthered? The answer is: only by means of religion, by belief in Ormazd and his cause. Belief must be not only theoretical, but practical. The believer must struggle for his cause, endeavouring to realise the good, both in nature and in human life. The important point to notice here is that the good spirit and his followers struggle in combination against the powers of evil, and that the final victory depends on the collaboration of God and men. This is the only religion in which the work of man is a condition of the victory of God over evil. Hence the religion of Zoroaster is in a unique sense the religion of morality. The struggle for the good is the duty required by the religion, and this duty can be fulfilled by moral action only.

Now what is the morality of the *Avesta?* It is certainly not pure morality in the modern sense. For it involves not only man's action towards his fellow man, but also action concerned with superstition inherited from a more primitive period. The duties of man here largely consist in the immediate fight with the evil spirits, especially in sacrifice and ritual. For the priesthood, the performance of the cult is nothing but a fight against the evil spirits, and a system of purifications to expel the evil spirits pervading nature and human life. Against these the pure elements, especially fire, are effective. The sacred fire is always kept burning as particularly potent in the capacity of a purifier. This conception is quite analogous to that, in Indian religion, of the god of Fire, Agni, who is specifically called the Purifier, *Pāvaka,* and drives away the demons, or *rākṣasas,* from the sacrifice.

In ordinary life a great many observances were in use for warding off evil spirits. Among these, cleansings were of great importance, because evil was regarded as a form of impurity, and these cleansings were also believed to have the power of expelling evil spirits. Water, for example, had a real anti-demoniac efficacy. This, again, is analogous to the Vedic idea that water washed away sin like a material substance. Again, after an illness all the bed-clothes had to be cleansed with extreme care in order to drive away the indwelling evil spirits. They did not know in those days that these demons were of an excessively minute order in the form of the germs of disease. Every sickness and the natural states of organic life, such as menstruation, were understood to belong to the great realm of death and devils. Many of the observances which, according to Persian ideas, were effective only as expelling the indwelling evil spirits, have a hygienic value. Ceremonial purification in fact often has a health-promoting result. According to the Zoroastrian view, every dead thing belonged to Ahriman, being both impure and causing impurity. Ritual cleansings were necessary after touching a dead dog, a dead human being, or any other dead body which when alive belonged to the realm of purity. By the way, it is only these that become impure by death: while the corpses of evil men and of noxious animals cause no impurity because the demon of death has left them.

The customs of mourning, further, imply throughout the expulsion of evil spirits, requiring the purification of the house, the family, and the district where the evil spirit of death has dwelt. As is well known, the Parsis at the present day bring the dead bodies of men and of dogs to the 'Towers of Silence,' where they are exposed to vultures and other carrion birds in order that the pure elements of earth, fire, or water should not be polluted by burial, cremation, or throwing into rivers. All such observances are but the moralization of very ancient superstitions concerning evil spirits, derived from the conceptions of uncivilized man. Quite similar ideas can be traced in Indian religion.

A minute comparison of the points in these and other respects which the ancient religions of Persia and India have in common would constitute a valuable study in comparative religion.

In the system of the *Avesta* everything suggestive of low vitality or injurious to life is regarded as the work of evil spirits. Hence unfruitfulness, cold, destructive heat, blight, weeds, noxious insects, harmful substances, and so forth have to be energetically combatted by man. This moral fight against evil leads to the advancement of civilization, which in Zarathuṣtra's time was of a pastoral and agricultural order. Hence it was the duty of the pious man to treat his cattle well and not to slay them for useless sacrifices. This care for cattle resulted in the sacred character of the cow, doubtless owing to the special utility of this animal. Veneration of the cow is evidently a very old conception, going back at any rate to the Indo-Aryan period, because it appears in the Vedic religion, and subsequently in an accentuated form. In the later *Avesta* frequent mention is also made of agricultural duties; here we learn that the cultivation of fields, the cutting of canals, the construction of roads and bridges, the building of houses, and the manufacture of agricultural implements are all important duties of the faithful. The weeding of the fields, the destruction of injurious insects and beasts are, we read, meritorious deeds, tending to efface the boundaries of Ahriman's dominion. The duties of an agricultural life constitute the religious ideals of the Persians, and the sacred texts continually furnish examples from agriculture, used to illustrate the holy life. Thus Ahura Mazda is represented as saying that the earth enjoys the best fortune in those regions where the believer grows most corn, and grass, and fruit; where he waters the dry soil and drains the damp: for that soil is not blessed which lies long uncultivated, waiting for a husbandman; but to him who works the soil with both arms will the earth yield riches. With this desire for cultivation goes the tendency to lay stress on its religious meritoriousness and its holy power. Thus in the *Vendīdād* we read: 'who sows corn sows holiness': and again: 'when the barley is arranged for threshing, the demons begin to sweat for fear; when the mill is arranged for grinding the barley, the demons lose their senses,' and so forth.

The standard of morality in the *Avesta* is the principle of utility: no useless action could here be regarded as moral. The conception of utility, however, often assumes an ideal character and reaches a high ethical level. Thus the productive activity of man is always highly esteemed, and nothing tending to curtail vitality in any direction is approved. We therefore never find any element of asceticism in the Zoroastrian religion. On the contrary it is the duty of every man to be healthy and vigorous that he may work effectively in the cause of righteousness. He is expected to marry and become the father of strong children; every act that could diminish the fertility of man is strictly forbidden. At the same time chastity was a necessary duty, and every sexual aberration was severely punished. In the later conflicts (after the 3rd cent. A.D.) with the Manichæans in Persia, the Zoroastrian priests carried on a controversy specially directed against the various forms of asceticism, such as celibacy, fasting, self-flagellation, and other forms of the mortification of the flesh. This is a clear indication how strongly the religion of Zoroaster was opposed to every form of asceticism. It is one of the very few religions in which this aspect of religion is absent.

The daily life of the priests was of course much taken up with the ritual matters of cleansing and exorcism; but these rites included many moral and educational elements, as the insistence on the duty of men to cleanse themselves from every defilement due to the devils, by the doing of useful works. It was the office of the priests to oversee and govern these multifarious exercises: it was in short their special task to uphold morality and educate the people in good works. In this system of training, the conception of sin as an inward state of mind is virtually absent as an element of the Avestan religion, sin being simply a transgression of the law. The deepest guilt from the religious point of view is unbelief, or in the extreme case, worship of the evil spirits. By the fulfilment of all duties every pious man or woman was regarded as able to produce a great store of merit for gaining the bliss of heaven, and very holy persons might be able to accumulate more than was needed for their own salvation. This surplus of merit is stored up in heaven as a kind of treasure to be distributed among the souls that are not sufficiently provided for. This belief is somewhat analogous to the Hindu view of *dharma* according to which religious merit is stored up in heaven, though in this case it is gradually used up by the producer himself, not transferred to others.

In this system there is a Final Judgment, in which good works decide. There are, however, two stages of judgment known even as early as the *gāthās*, the oldest part of the *Avesta*. The one is a scrutiny of individual souls; the other is a trial of mankind as a whole.

The individual judgment takes place before the tribunal of Mithra, where the souls are weighed in the balance of the spirits, without bias towards the righteous or against the wicked. Even the acquitted soul is punished for its evil deeds by the Angel Aṣa ; it may then cross the Bridge of Judgment, called Chinvat, which leads to heaven. The guilty, on the other hand, fall from this bridge into the gulf of hell below.

The Final Judgment takes place on the last Day, when the bodily resurrection comes to pass, and the souls, blessed and wicked alike, are joined to their bodies. This judgment is an immense ordeal: resurrected mankind will be required to pass through the molten metal which will then overflow the whole earth. The fire will burn very fiercely for the wicked, but very mildly for the good. It will in all cases destroy every remnant of impurity, leaving man as well as the entire earth in that complete state of purity and holiness which was its original state before Ahriman introduced his defilements. The final judgment has much of the character of a natural process of cleansing by the purifying agency of fire. But in the individual judgment the formal element of a legal procedure appears: we have here the principle of merciless retribution, for the god Mithra has merely the duty of superintending the procedure, while the supreme god Ahura Mazda has no part to play in it at all, the idea of mercy being absolutely excluded from the accomplishment of human destiny. Retribution is here as inevitable as in the Indian doctrine of *karma*; but it is inexorable judgment as compared with inexorable fate.

The religious community has, however, the power in Zoroastrianism of releasing men from the consequences of their guilt by means of the confession of guilt made at the moment of death, and by the sacramental means of putting the holy juice of *haoma* into the ear of the dying man. But such dispensations are possible only in virtue of the surplus of good works at the disposal of the community as a whole.

Now as regards the general level of ancient Persian morality, it was not merely external and mechanical, for righteousness came to be understood not only as outward purity and practical deeds, but as the true realization of right conduct in life. If we analyze their moral system in detail, we find that from the personal point of view the duties held in greatest regard were self-control, temperance, economy, the keeping of early hours, industry, assiduity in practical affairs; and the social virtues considered necessary to the life of the community are truthfulness, faithfulness, uprightness, justice, generosity and harmony. These virtues are also demanded as qualities that ought to be inherent in the highest type of Persian manhood. In the Pahlavi books there is a list of thirty-three duties, which represent a very refined moral outlook, combined, however, with a remnant of primitive social custom. In the *Vendīdād* the system of penalties, which apply in the moral law of the *Avesta* as taught by the priests is codified. We see here how the conception of morality in the *Avesta* is essentially a juristic one. It is conformity to the law. Religion in the *Avesta* is called law: and the

Persian could not distinguish between the two ideas of law and religion. It is much the same with the conception of *dharma* in ancient India, and with the "Law" in Judaism. The moral system of Zoroastrianism was not based on man's love for his neighbour. The monotonous and somewhat mechanical opposition of good and evil left little room for the consideration of the intermediate stages of real life, or for the emotions of disinterestedness in the moral outlook of the ancient Persians.

There was little chance of the sphere of morality extending in Avestic times to international relations. For at that time and long after the Persians were in constant conflict on their borders with the alien race of the Turanians, whose predatory nomadic manner of life was necessarily repugnant to an advanced people like the Persians with their agricultural civilization and alien religion, and who in the eyes of the Persians would be unbelievers. In any case, there is no reason to believe that the ancient Persians were less isolated from or less hostile to the neighbouring peoples than were other nations of antiquity.

Selected Bibliography.

Darmesteter, *Le Zend-Avesta*, Paris, 1892-3; tr. of the *Vendidād*, in *Sacred Books of the East*, Vol. iv, Oxford, 1895. Williams Jackson, *Iranische Religion* in *Grundriss der Iranischen Philologie*. Lehmann, *Zarathuṣtra*, Copenhagen, 1899-1902.

LECTURE III.

THE RELIGIONS OF INDIA.

A. Brahmanism.

We now come to the religion of ancient India, which is more closely akin to that of ancient Persia than any other. For both are descended from the one faith of the Indo-Iranian branch of the Aryan race, at the time when they still lived as one people in a part of what is now Persia, before the Indians branched off to migrate into India by the north-west. Had this pre-historic religion in its separate development in Bactria, not been dislocated by the reform of Zoroaster, the old Persian religion would have been as like that of the *Rigveda*, as the language of the *Avesta* is like that of the *Rigveda*; specialists know that whole verses of the *Avesta* can be turned word for word into Vedic, by the simple application of phonetic laws, so as to produce lines which are not only correct in form but in poetic spirit. This Vedic religion is not only the oldest of the Aryan religions, but is also the only Aryan religion which, in its later form of Hinduism, is still the prevailing religion in its original home. This Vedic religion is peculiarly important as a branch of study. It is not only the earliest body of religious beliefs preserved in a literary guise, but also presents a more primitive phase of religious thought than is recorded in any other literature. It can, moreover, be followed downwards step by step through all the various stages of its development. It is finally the source of the religion of the modern Hindus, which can thus be historically traced backwards throughout a period of no less than 3,500 years. No other religion therefore furnishes such invaluable material for the study of the historical evolution of religious thought. As a natural result of its high value as a training ground to the investigator of religions, the study of Vedic religion gave birth, in the latter half of the 19th century to the science of Comparative Religion. Lectures on Comparative Religion are therefore peculiarly appropriate in the country which is the home of the Veda. The study of the Vedas further led to the production, under the editorship of Max Müller, of that monumental collection, in 50 volumes, of translations of all the most important *Sacred Books of the East*, a mine of material for the comparative investigation of early religions. Perhaps the most valuable feature of Comparative Religion is, that it enables us to ascertain, by scientific method, what the various religions have in common, thus leading to enlightenment to the removal of prejudice, and in this way to the advancement of civilization. I do not think that any other study can be so valuable in this respect. Another important feature of this science is that it acts as a check on wild preconceived speculations about the age and growth of various religious and mythological conceptions. It has, in fact, much the same value as comparative philology (which by the way originated from the study of Sanskrit) has in controlling extravagant etymologies. Without the Vedic evidence we should not know, for instance, what was the original nature of the Greek gods, whom we meet with only at a late anthropomorphic stage of development. That evidence, however, shows that many at least of the Greek gods must have been personifications of natural phenomena : the evidence of Greek mythology alone could not prove this. It also shows us, along with the corroborative evidence of comparative philology, what lay behind the religion of the Indo-Aryans, and what religious material they brought with them from the antecedent period of national existence. In this way only do we know that before the Indo-Aryans entered India from the north-west, they formed with the Persians a single Indo-Iranian people, who had many ritual practices as well as religious and mythological notions in common, representing an earlier phase of thought. Thus we know that in that prehistorical period, they performed sacrifice (Vedic *yajña*, Avestic *yasna*); that they already had various kinds of priests (*hotar*=*zaotar*; *atharvan*=*athrāvan* 'fire-priest'); that they had the conception of cosmic and ritual order, of natural and moral law (*ṛta=aṣa*); that they already had a sacred drink (*soma=haoma*), the intoxicating juice of the Soma plant offered as the main oblation, pressed between two stones, purified by a sieve, mixed with milk, described as the lord of plants, as growing on the mountains, and as brought down to men by an eagle or eagles. Their highest gods were called *asura=ahura*, conceived as mighty kings, drawn through the air on their war chariots by swift steeds, in character benevolent and almost entirely free from guile and immoral traits. They also had a fire-cult. They worshipped a sun-god *Mitra=Mithra*; invoked the waters (*Āpaḥ=āpo*); the Wind (*vāyu=vayu*); a deity called the 'son of waters' (*apām napāt=apam napāt*); a divine being connected with Soma (*Gandharva=Gandarewa*); *Indra Vṛtrahan*, the demon-slaying god Indra, who appears in the *Avesta* in the somewhat altered capacity of a demon Indra and a genius of victory *Verethragna* (a change doubtless caused by the mythological dislocation produced by Zarathuṣtra's religious reform); a ruler of the dead: the Vedic Yama, son of Vivasvant=Yima, son of Vivahvant, ruler of Paradise. They also had a highly ethical god, represented by the Vedic Varuṇa and the Avestic Ahura Mazda, the 'wise spirit,' who are parallel in character, though not in name. We should find the affinity in the domain of mythology much greater between Veda and *Avesta*, had not the religious reform of Zarathuṣtra, which of course took place after the separation of the Persian and Indian branches, brought about a very considerable displacement and transformation of mythological conceptions in the Iranian religion. If we possessed Avestan literature dating from before the reform, the approximation would thus evidently have been much greater.

Comparative mythology, which also arose from the study of the Veda, further indicates that the Veda derives a heritage from the far older Indo-European period, when the remote ancestors of the various branches of the Indo-Europeans still formed one single people. But the information we can here gather is much scantier and less certain. We know, however, at least that they already believed in celestial gods (Skt. *devas*, Lith. *devas*, Lat. *deus* : from *div* 'heaven'); and that one of them was the personification of heaven, the Vedic *Dyaus* and the phonetically equivalent Greek Zeus (= *Dyeus*). The latter, the chief of the Olympian gods of Greece, is much more anthropomorphic, more like a human being than Dyaus, who is, however, at least thought of as a father. For in the *Rig-veda* he is addressed as *Dyauṣ pitar*, 'O Father Heaven,' as also in Greek Ζευ πατερ and Latin *Jūpiter*. You remember that in China, Heaven is the chief deity. The earth is, moreover called a mother : this is the case both in the *Rigv da* and in the Greek religion. The two are often invoked together in the hymns of *Rigveda* in the dual as *Dyāvā-pṛthivī*. This idea of Heaven and Earth being universal parents probably goes back to a still remoter antiquity. For it is familiar to the mythology of China, as I have already mentioned, and of New Zealand, and may be traced in that of Egypt. It was possibly a universal belief of primitive man. The practice of magical rites and the worship of inanimate objects, which still survive in the Veda, probably come down from an equally remote stage in the mental development of mankind. Some elements, however, especially those which do not appear in the earliest period, such as the adoration of serpents, phallus-worship, and the belief in transmigration, the Indo-Aryans may have borrowed from the aborigines of India with whom they came in contact ; for India is the land of snakes; phallus-worshippers are spoken of as unbelievers ; while the transmigration belief cannot be traced in any of the Vedic Saṁhitās, and is not known in the other Indo-European religions.

1. I may now proceed to describe the nature of the Vedic gods and of man's relation to them, as throwing light on the moral conceptions of the age. The Vedic religion was polytheistic, the worship of many gods, who were largely personifications of the powers of nature, such as Sun, Wind, Fire. Their number is stated in the *Rigveda* to be thirty-three ;

but we find not more than about twenty of these ordinarily invoked. They are conceived as human in appearance, each having one head and two arms. The anthropomorphic character is always more developed in the deities that date from a pre-Indian period, such as Indra and Varuṇa. The home of the gods is heaven, where exhilarated by their favourite drink, Soma, they live a life of bliss. Their most characteristic attribute is power: they regulate the order of nature (*ṛta*) and vanquish the powers of evil. They rule over all creatures; no man can thwart their ordinances; and the fulfilment of desires is dependent on them. They are also benevolent, bestowing prosperity on mankind, the only one in whom injurious traits appear being Rudra. They are 'true' and 'not deceitful.' They are friends and protectors of the honest and righteous, but punish guilt and sin. They are thus moral. But their morality of course only reflects the ethical standard of an early stage of civilization. The best representative is Varuṇa, who as a moral governor stands far above the other gods. Omniscient, he is the upholder of physical and moral order. Sin, which is the infringement of his ordinances, arouses his wrath, and is severely punished by him. He binds sinners with his fetters. A hater and punisher of falsehood, he is merciful to the penitent. He releases men not only from the sins they themselves commit, but from those committed by their fathers. He spares the suppliant who daily infringes his laws, and is gracious to those who have broken his ordinances by thoughtlessness. There is no hymn addressed to Varuṇa that does not contain a prayer for forgiveness of guilt. The element of divine mercy, you see, thus finds a place in the Vedic religion, but as you remember, was completely excluded in the Avestic system owing to the juristic character of that religion. Though Varuṇa is the most moral of the gods, his alliance with righteousness is not such as to prevent him from employing craft against the hostile and deceitful man. On the whole, moral elevation is less prominent in the character of the gods than greatness and power. Various features of the earth's surface, besides artificial objects, are found deified in the *Rigveda*. Mountains are often addressed as divinities, and various rivers, the Sindhu (Indus), the Vipāś (Biās), the Śutudrī (Sutlej), and especially the Sarasvatī, are invoked in several hymns. Plants, the sacrificial post, the pressing stones, and weapons are addressed in other hymns. The powers of evil are represented by demons, the aerial foes of the gods, who fight against them. The combat is regularly between a single god and a single demon, generally between Indra and Vṛtra. Later, in the period of the Brāhmaṇas, the fight is regularly between the gods as a whole, and the demons, now called Asuras, as a whole. This mythological conflict was, as you remember, moralized in the religion of the *Avesta*, as a conflict between the principle of the good, as Ahura Mazda, and that of evil, as Angra Mainyu. There are besides many lower or terrestrial demons, generally called *Rakṣasas*, the enemies of men.

It will, I think, be of interest at this point to pause and consider the position of polytheism in the various religions that I am treating in these lectures. All of them, except Christianity, have a background of polytheism. Some retain polytheism throughout, but even these always show some development. Among the Vedic gods, one, Varuṇa, is distinctly superior to the others, though not to the extent of being a chief god. In the Chinese popular religion, which is polytheistic, Heaven is the highest god. The polytheistic Greek and Roman religions, have Heaven as their highest god, Zeus and Jūpiter (=*dyaus*). The Iranian god Ahura, once very much the same as Varuṇa, was by the reform of Zoroaster, almost transformed into a monotheistic god, only that, unwilling to make a good god responsible for the creation of evil in the world, he placed the power of Evil in opposition to him in the dualistic system of the *Avesta*. In Judaism and Islam, the chief god, having ousted polytheism, became the one god of the nation. Christianity alone has not any background of polytheism, because it is the daughter of an earlier religion, which was already monotheistic. The Vedic religion in its Brāhmaṇa period made some advance towards a chief god in Prajāpati, the creator, but this tendency never led to monotheism in India. On the other hand, the Vedic religion developed the incipient identification of the gods with one another and with nature into the one pantheistic world-soul of the Vedānta system. This is the only one of the various religions that has developed a system of pantheism. The only other one that might have done so was the popular Chinese religion, which you remember I defined as a 'universalistic animism,' if this religion had been taken in hand by philosophy.

The relation of the worshipper to the gods in the *Rigveda* is generally speaking one of dependence on their will. Prayers and sacrifices are offered to win their favour or deprecate their anger. The expectation of something in return for the offering is often evidentt, the prevailing tone of many a hymn being 'I give to thee that you mayest give to me.' The benefits sought are not always material ones, the forgiveness of the gods being often implored. The sacrifice offered to them consists in milk, butter, grain, or the flesh of sheep, goats, and cattle. It is conveyed them in heaven by the god of fire, or they come down in their cars to receive it on a bed of grass prepared for their reception.

The idea is, moreover, frequently expressed in the *Rigveda* that hymns, sacrifices, and especially offerings of Soma increase the strength and valour of the gods. This idea tended to raise the influence of the priests and to encourage their sacerdotal pretensions, which gradually went on growing during the Vedic age. Thus we find the statement in the *White Yajurveda* that the Brahman who possesses correct knowledge has the gods in his power. By the time of the Brāhmaṇas, the sacrifice had come to be regarded as all-powerful, controlling not only the gods, but the very processes of nature, such as sunrise. The gods were no longer addressed in hymns as new and spontaneous utterances, but with spells applied along with an elaborate ritual for the purpose of compelling the gods to comply with the wishes of the worshipper. The appeal was no longer of the nature of a prayer, but consisted of formulas of a mechanical and magical order. The moral attitude of man towards the divine powers had by this time very greatly deteriorated: religion had, as Andrew Lang wittily expressed it, fallen into its sacerdotage.

2. Let us now turn to the moral side of the Vedic religion as manifested in the relation of man to his neighbour. We do not of course find any systematic account of the moral ideas of the age in the Vedas, but a fairly complete picture can nevertheless be pieced together from the incidental references and allusions contained in the hymns. There is sufficient evidence of this kind to show that marriage was an established institution, apparently of a more permanent order than it was among some of the other branches of the Aryan race even in later times. Monogamy was the ordinary practice, as can be seen by various allusions in the wedding hymn of the *Rigveda*. The position of women was, moreover, one of much greater freedom than in later times. There was no such thing as the seclusion of women, which came about in India as the result of the Mohammedan invasion some two thousand years later. It is, however, clear that the number of wives was not restricted to one in Vedic times, because co-wives (*sa-patnī*) are frequently mentioned, and the *Rigveda* itself contains spells to enable a woman to gain her husband's affections in preference to her rival wives. The family was evidently the foundation of society, as we have seen it to have been even in the savage stage of humanity. Parental affection and filial piety are often referred to, as for instance in the very first hymn of the *Rigveda*: 'Be easy of access to us, O Agni, as a father is to his son'; or as, in a funeral hymn, Earth is besought to cover up the deceased as a mother her son with the end of her garment. There is no evidence to show that daughters were ever married before the age of puberty had

9

arrived. Some are even spoken of as 'aging at home,' which indicates that marriage was not regarded as a necessity. The birth of daughters is deprecated in the *Atharvaveda*, but abundance of sons is constantly prayed for in the Vedic period, while lack of sons is regarded as on the same level as poverty, adoption being considered a mere makeshift. The wife holds a more honoured position in the Rigvedic period than in that of the Brāhmaṇas, for she shares with her husband in the offering of sacrifice.

The standard of sexual morality must have been comparatively high, for adultery and rape were considered serious crimes, and illegitimate births were concealed.

The commonest crime seems to have been robbery, generally in the form of cattle-lifting, and practised during darkness.

In several respects the religion and morality of the Vedic period still lacked features which are conspicuous in later Brahmanism. Thus the sacredness of life was as yet by no means prominent. At a period when the Indo-Aryans were spreading through the country by warlike conquest and enemies were constantly being slain, respect for human life could not have been great. Again, there is some reason to believe that though the primitive custom of widow-burning had not died out, it was restricted to the warrior caste; while much later it was a universal practice in India. Moreover, later Brahmanism, as represented by the code of Manu, the *Mahābhārata*, and many other productions of what is called classical Sanskrit, shows two momentous changes that revolutionized the religious and social system of the Indo-Aryans: the doctrine of *karma* and transmigration on the one hand, and the system of caste on the other. These two together have given to Indian civilization its special stamp for 2,500 years. In the Vedas, though reference is made to the joys of heaven and to the tortures of hell, thus indicating in a general way that good deeds are rewarded and evil deeds punished, there is no allusion to the doctrine of rebirth. The Upanishads, however, the latest phase of the Brāhmaṇas, mention the rebirth of virtuous men as Brahmins and others of high position, and of wicked men as dogs, swine, or Chandālas. The idea of *karma*, or retributory action, and *karma-vipāka*, or 'ripening of acts' in future births, pervades the six systems of philosophy and the earliest law-books of the *dharmasūtra* class. A result of the combined doctrine of transmigration and *karma* is, it is true, to reconcile men to their fate as the just retribution for deeds done in a previous life, but on the other hand it paralyzes action, drives to asceticism, and makes action self-regarding, since it becomes the aim of every man to win salvation for himself individually, by acquiring the right knowledge. There is consequently little scope for the development of other-regarding virtues, as each individual is intent on gaining his own salvation. Thus it is that none of the six philosophical systems includes a section on morality. What the Dharmasūtras say about moral duties is of a narrow type, because they state only the special duties of men as determined by their rebirth in a particular caste, especially the Brahmin caste. They also discuss the obligations of Brahmin ascetics who, by keeping the five vows of non-injury to living beings, of abstention from theft, of truthfulness, of continence, of liberality, and by the practice of various austerities, and by concentration of mind, endeavour to obtain full deliverance from the bonds of *karma*, and to reach final emancipation by absorption in the supreme soul. Several of the duties in this list are self-regarding. The doctrine of *ahiṃsā*, or non-injury to living beings, spread considerably during this period, not so much perhaps owing to the growth of other-regarding morality, as from the fear that relatives might be embodied in the particular creature that was being injured.

Again, the establishment of an elaborate system of caste which characterizes Indian civilization from this time onwards, has had a narrowing influence on the social virtues, and has arrested their development. For instead of unifying the population it tended to split it up into innumerable groups divided by insurmountable barriers which forbade intermarriage and eating together, thus limiting the application of other-regarding morality. It further fostered the arrogance of the higher castes, especially of the Brahmins, who constantly endeavoured to enforce their claims to spiritual and social superiority. On the other hand, it tended to the degradation of the lower castes, whose contact, or even mere shadow, might cause impurity.

An injurious effect of the caste system was, moreover, the custom of child-marriage resulting from the prohibition of marrying outside the caste and the consequent difficulty of obtaining suitable husbands. A further disadvantageous effect was that, in such early marriages, the young people had no say in the matter, and that the frequent premature consummation of marriage tended to the production of immature children and the consequent deterioration of physique in the population.

Speaking generally, the moral code and the notions as to right and wrong prevailing during this period in India did not differ essentially from those current among other nations of antiquity. Distinctive features were the peculiar sanctity attributed to Brahmins as well as all their belongings, and to the cow, the sacred animal of the Hindus. The veneration of the cow can, however, be traced back to the Indo-Iranian period; for, as I have already pointed out, this was also a feature, though in a less developed form, of the Zoroastrian religion.

By the performance of a penance every sin could be atoned for, and these penances were an important source of profit for the Brahmins, much in the same way as dispensations were to the Roman Catholic Church during the Middle Ages in Europe. This system of atonement goes back to the

Indo-Iranian period, for the penances prescribed in the *Vendīdād* of the *Avesta* are closely analogous to the penances (*prāyaścittam*) of the Sanskrit law-books. Thus one who has committed the mortal sin of drinking intoxicating liquor is required to drink the same liquor when boiling hot. For certain forms of stealing, the lunar penance (*cāndrāyaṇa*), a severe form of fasting, is prescribed. Swallowing the five products of the cow (*pañca-gavyam*) is part of the penance for various offences; it has, I am told, been reduced to a very minute quantity for the heinous offence of crossing the sea. The *Viṣṇu-sūtra* states that scratching the back of a cow destroys all guilt. Religious gifts to Brahmins are greatly recommended as penances. Several instances are recorded in Indian history of rich men giving their own weight in gold or silver to Brahmins, a practice called *tulā-puruṣa*, 'a man's weight.'

Though each class had its special duties assigned to it, there were also general obligations common to all cases, some self-regarding, others social: of the former kind were self-restraint, purity, contentment, of the latter kind, veracity, liberality, sympathy, straightforwardness, obedience towards elders, regard for animal life. The doctrine of *ahiṁsā* was, however, not so much insisted on in the Brahmanic as in the Buddhist and Jaina creeds: for a sacrifice, cattle may be slain, and the meat of such cattle may be eaten, although the doctrine of *karma* and of the soul's passage through all kinds of animal bodies, according to its deeds in a former life, is fully recognized in the code of Manu.

Asceticism, combined with religious meditation, occupies an important position in Hinduism. The fourth stage (*āśrama*) in the life of the Brahmin is that of the religious mendicant (*yati*), which is preceded by that of the forest hermit (*vānaprastha*). These are laid down as regular orders into which the Brahmin should successively enter.

The *Mahābhārata*, like the legal codes, forms a vast

thesaurus of Hindu ethics. It represents perhaps more truly the actual standard of morality prevailing at the period, than do the law-books, the standard of which tends to be ideal and artificial, and which, being written by Brahmins for Brahmins, are apt to exaggerate their caste pretensions. The epic, in a general way, describes the path of religious duty as eightfold (which it is also said to be in Buddhism), but here this path is stated to consist in sacrifice, penance, study, self-control, absence of greed, liberality, mercy, and truthfulness. It is the epics that furnish pictures of what the domestic and social life of the times must have been. In these, wives appear as loyal and devoted to their husbands, as Damayantī and Sāvitrī, while husbands are affectionately disposed towards their wives. Parents are fondly attached to their children and are ready to sacrifice themselves for their welfare. Children are dutiful to their parents and submissive to their superiors. Love and harmony prevail throughout the family circle.

Though, as I have already remarked, morality does not come within the range of the six orthodox systems of Hindu philosophy, as it does within that of the canonical books of the unorthodox system of Buddhism, a moralizing tone pervades the whole range of Sanskrit literature. It is particularly strong in the collections of fables, like the *Pañca-tantra* and the *Hitopadeśa*, which are to a large extent treatises on morality (*nīti*) inculcated through instructive speeches put into the mouths of tigers, jackals, cats, parrots, monkeys, and other animals. It also pervades the Sanskrit lyrics and dramas, among which the *Prabodhacandrodaya*, is an example of an allegorical and philosophical play which may be compared with some of the old English 'Moralities.' It is not too much to say that in no literature is the moralizing note so prominent. It is perhaps just owing to the universality of this mode of expression that there are so few works in Sanskrit dealing with morality exclusively. The key-note of all this poetry is the doctrine of the vanity of human life, which, developing before the rise of Buddhism, has dominated Indian thought ever since. The only true happiness is here represented as to be found in the abandonment of desire and retirement from the world. The poet turns from the beauties of nature with sadness to seek mental calm and lasting happiness in the solitude of the forest. Hence the pious anchorite living in contemplation is often enthusiastically described. But renunciation is not the only goal to which the fleeting nature of worldly existence leads these poets. The necessity of pursuing virtue is another practical lesson they draw from it. Gentleness and forbearance towards good and bad is recommended after the example of the moon who does not withdraw her light even from the hut of the outcast. The spirit of universal tolerance and love of mankind appears when we read that 'even a Śūdra deserves respect who knows and does his duty well,' or that 'noble-minded men regard the whole world as their kin.' The value of true friendship and of intercourse with good men is often dwelt on. The conception of fate is naturally often touched upon in this poetry. We frequently read that no one can escape from the operation of destiny, but that this should not paralyze human effort. For, it is pointed out, since fate is nothing else than the result of action done in a former birth, every man can by right conduct shape his future fate, just as a potter can mould a lump of clay into whatever form he likes.

When we come down to later times, we find a general tendency on the part of religious founders, such as Basava, the founder of the Lingāyats, in the 12th century, Kabir the founder of the Kabir-panthis, in the 15th, of Nānak and of Chaitanya in the 16th, to proclaim the social equality of all those who entered their order, so as to relax the bonds of caste. In practice, however, it has turned out that this levelling down of caste distinctions has met with only partial and temporary success.

As regards the present day, we find in the Census reports

of 1901 some interesting attempts to establish the actual standard of morality in India. The conclusions arrived at are these. The ordinary Hindu knows it is wrong to commit murder, adultery, theft, and perjury, or to be covetous. He honours his parents, in the case of his father at any rate, to a degree exceeding the customs of nearly all other nations, which have no ceremony resembling that of the *Śrāddha* or funeral offering, except, you will remember, the Chinese. The influence of caste here is of the utmost importance: the principal sanction attaching to a breach of morality seems to be the fear of caste penalties rather than the fear of divine punishment. In the case of perjury, the offence may be committed, without public disapproval, on behalf of a caste-fellow, or even an inhabitant of the same village. The doctrine of *karma* is stated to be one of the firmest beliefs of all classes of Hindus, and the fear that a man shall reap as he has sown, is an appreciable element in the average morality. As for heaven and hell, they are not regarded, it is stated, as merely transitory stages of existence in the cycle of transmigration (*saṁsāra*), but the soul when sufficiently purified goes to dwell in heaven for ever. There is no idea of absorption in the supreme soul whose place is far above.

The belief in metempsychosis, it appears, does not prevail all over India. Thus in the words of the Central Provinces Report, 'the ordinary Hindu peasant has practically no belief in the transmigration of souls, but has a vague idea that there is a future life, in which those who are good in this world will be happy in heaven (*sarg* Skt. *svarga*), whilst those who are bad will be wretched in hell (*narak*).' The general effect, however, of these two different beliefs on the state of morality remains the same, the idea of retribution in a future state being common to both of them.

The influence of Christian morality on the religious life of India began to manifest itself, during the 19th century, in the teaching and practical working of the various theistical sects called *samāj*: the Ārya and the Brahma Samāj. Thus the Ārya Samāj insists on the education of both sexes, the percentage of literacy being consequently high in this community as compared with the rest of the population. One of its aims, too, is to do good to the world by improving the physical, intellectual, spiritual, moral, and social condition of mankind.

It is in the teaching of these communities that we can see the advance of morality so as to include its widest circle, the good of humanity as a whole. It is true that as a result of the caste system, the solidarity of the family group is greater than in any other system of society; but it has, otherwise, been still less possible for orthodox Hinduism than for nearly all other early religions, with its caste barriers, to overstep the rigid divisions of society and the frontiers of national morality. It is true that advanced individual thinkers occasionally expressed cosmopolitan ideas, but it is doubtful whether, owing to their extremely limited geographical and ethnological knowledge, even the most enlightened Hindus, except in quite recent times, really extended such sentiments to peoples beyond the frontiers of *Bharatavarṣa*, the Sanskrit name for India.

Selected Bibliography.

Barth, *The Religions of India*, London, 1890. Hopkins, *Religions of India*, London, 1896. Macdonell, *Vedic Mythology*, in *Grundriss der Indo-Arischen Philologie*, Strassburg, 1897; *Vedic Religion*, in Hastings' *Encyclopædia of Religion and Ethics*, xii, pp. 601-18, Edinburgh, 1921. *Reports of the Census of India*, 1921.

LECTURE IV

Buddhism and Buddhist Morality

Buddhism is essentially an Indian religion, being an offshoot of Brahmanism and deriving many details from that system; it has nevertheless become a fundamentally different faith. Founded by Buddha in north-eastern India towards the end of the 6th century B.C., it disappeared, like Christianity, from its native country many centuries ago, but became one of the three great world-religions, profoundly influencing the civilization of the Farther East, as Christianity has influenced that of the West. In India itself, Buddhism deeply affected the spiritual life of the country for over a thousand years. All its canonical texts, both Pāli and Sanskrit, were produced in India; the Buddhism of the many countries to which this religion has spread could not be understood without a knowledge of its earliest or Indian phase; and without the evidence of Buddhist architecture and sculpture in India the history of Indian art would be impossible.

The original and essential doctrine of Buddhism is that all earthly existence is suffering, the only means of release from it being renunciation and eternal death. Brahmanism being its basis, the essential features of Buddhism cannot be fully understood without a definite statement, as to which of the religious ideas of the antecedent religion it rejected, and which of them it retained. On the one hand, Buddha repudiated the authority of the Vedas and the Vedic sacrificial system; he condemned self-mortification; he denied the existence both of a world-soul and of the individual soul; he discarded the distinctions of caste within the monastic order, though not as a general classification of society; and he was entirely averse from speculation on metaphysical problems, to which the adherents of Brahmanism were so prone. On the other hand, Buddha retained the belief in transmigration (*saṃsāra*) and retribution (*karma*) practically unchanged; he also adhered to the doctrine that the great goal of endeavour is release from transmigration, to be attained by means of renunciation. Even the fundamental doctrine of Buddhism on its philosophical side, that all earthly existence is suffering, is only a development of the view of life already apparent in the Upanishads. The Sāṃkhya philosophy, which is the most pessimistic of all the Brahmanic systems, may in its earliest form have contributed to the foundations of the philosophical side of Buddhism. It is really only on what may be called its religious side that Buddhism is original. Primitive Buddhism was a religion of humanity, a system of practical morality, the keynote of which is universal charity: kindness to all beings, animals as well as men. It is here that the originality of Buddha's teaching is chiefly to be found; for the sphere of ethics had been neglected by Brahmin thought, which was mainly directed to ritual and theosophical speculation. To this aspect of Buddhism is to be traced the profound influence which it has exercised as a world-religion.

In contrast with Brahmin morality, which consists in conformity to an impersonal law and tradition, that of Buddhism is bound up with the personality of its founder. This is a necessary consequence of the starting-point of the religion. Buddha is revered not only as the founder of the religion, but also as the revealer of final truths and the guide of all beings to the same attainment as his own. He is the Saviour, the ferryman who conducts men to the farther shore of perfection; which may be reached by all who follow his instructions in accordance with truth. Buddha's position in Buddhism is similar to that of Christ in Christianity, as is already indicated by the very names of these two religions as called after their founders. Buddha is the exemplar whom all must follow who desire to obtain salvation. His person is the pivot on which all Buddhist thought turns, the ideal at which every believer should aim. In him personal perfection is united with universal truths. Thus he is represented in the *Itivuttaka* as saying of himself 'one who sees me sees the truth.' He is the light of the world (or its eye, *loka-chakkhu*), but everyone should discover the same light in himself (*atta-dīpa*), the Master being the revealer of the light and not an intruder from the outside. One takes refuge in the Buddha in order to take refuge in himself (*atta-saraṇa*), as the master has done. The whole of the doctrines of early Buddhism are set forth in the fundamental four noble truths. The first three represent the philosophical, the fourth the religious aspect of the system. These four truths are the following.

(1) All that exists is subject to suffering. This at once shows the thoroughly pessimistic character of the Buddhist outlook. The Buddhist scriptures constantly dwell on the transitoriness and worthlessness of all things, and no other religion is so penetrated by the belief in the utter vanity and misery of existence.

(2) The second truth is: the origin of suffering is human passions. Suffering is described as resulting from thirst (*tṛṣṇā*, Pāli *tanhā*) or the desire of life, which until it is destroyed, leads to continued transmigration and the return of suffering. 'Thirst' by the formula of causation is traced backward through a chain of several causes to *avidyā*, 'ignorance,' that is, lack of knowledge of the doctrine of Buddha. From 'thirst' arises 'attachment' to worldly objects. This leads to continued 'becoming' (*bhava*), an infinite series of new existences. These, finally, are the cause of birth, old age, and death, pain, suffering, sorrow, and despair.

What was called soul was regarded by Buddha only as an aggregate of changing individual elements, not as eternal and unchangeable, different and separable from the body.

(3) The third noble truth is: the cessation of passions releases from suffering.

With Buddha's view of the soul is closely connected that of *Nirvāṇa*, which means 'extinction' like that of a lamp. This is of two kinds, representing two stages of release. (1) The first, which is a necessary antecedent of the second, is the extinction of desire (*tṛṣṇā*), resulting in 'blissful calm' during the remainder of life (corresponding to the *jīvan-mukti*, 'deliverance while alive' of the Brahmins). The enlightenment now attained causes the cessation of ignorance and consequently of re-birth, but the results of deeds done before enlightenment have to be suffered while the released man is still alive. (2) The second stage is not reached till decease, after which there is no awakening, transmigration is at an end, and birth and death are overcome without a remainder. This is *Parinirvāṇa* or 'complete extinction,' often inaccurately spoken of simply as *Nirvāṇa*.

It is sometimes thought that Buddha avoided a clear definition of complete *Nirvāṇa*, because he often puts aside the question of what the exact condition after death is when release has been obtained. But he appears to have done this because he considered the question immaterial, the main object of his doctrine being deliverance from suffering. He left no doubt as to the goal to which his teaching led: the cessation of all the *saṃskāras*, impressions of former acts, and annihilation of all the *skandhas*, the elements of existence, *i. e.*, eternal death. The glowing colours, however, in which the bliss enjoyed in the first or living stage of release is described, led to the transformation of complete *Nirvāṇa* into a positive paradise in Sanskrit Buddhism.

These first three noble truths are concerned with the philosophical side of Buddha's teaching, and were meant for the learned only. It was the fourth truth, which embraces practical morality and was meant for the people, that made Buddhism the religion it became. This fourth truth is the following.

(4) The path that leads to the cessation of suffering is the eightfold path. This truth represents the sum total of Buddhist morality, which is coloured by the goal to which it leads. The eightfold path comprises: right belief, right resolve, right word, right deed, right life, right endeavour, right thought, right meditation.

It should here be remembered that, in the Buddhist view, practical morality should be accompanied by theoretical knowledge, and that the combined moral and intellectual perfection of a personality is the highest aim of Buddhist ethics. Mere knowledge, or a solitary immersion in mystic contemplation without practical actions, is not perfection, while on the other hand morality without insight into the depth of truth is baseless; in other words morality unsupported by reason has no solid foundation (that is, it is the customary morality of the ignorant).

Many of you will probably remember in this connection the Sanskrit aphorism which expresses a similar idea: 'knowledge without action is a mere burden, like a necklace on an ugly woman.'

(*i*) The first stage of the eightfold path is *true belief*. It is, of course, indispensable to all who enter on the path of salvation, but especially for the monk who has renounced the world. As the cardinal maxim of Buddhist morality is, to abandon the false and base conduct of common men, and to adopt the methods of Buddha, in whose person is to be found the guide to the ultimate end, the important rôle which faith fills in Buddhist morality is obvious. It is indeed one of the cardinal virtues of Buddhism, just as it is in Christianity.

The next five stages comprise the five commandments prescribed for laymen and practically all of them including man's duty to his neighbour. The cardinal virtue dominating them all is charity (in St. Paul's sense of 'human kindness,' *maitrī* in Sanskrit, *metta* in Pāli): which Buddha declared to be of far greater value than all other means of acquiring religious merit, and the practice of which is constantly emphasized in the Buddhist scriptures. One of the precepts inculcated in connection with *metta*, or human kindness, is to requite evil with good. The history of Buddhism shows that such precepts were actually practised. This precept resulting from charity was also preached by Christ. You will remember that Confucius would not go as far as this: he asserted that evil should be requited with justice, not with good. That the standard of the moral law in Buddhism is very high is evident from the five commandments.

(*ii*) 1. The first is 'Thou shalt not kill.' The meaning conveyed by the prohibition is that one should refrain, not only from taking life directly or indirectly, but from doing harm to creatures both strong and weak. With the desire to avoid crushing insects and the shoots of plants was connected the practice of remaining in the monasteries during the rains. For similar reasons the Buddhists abominated the animal sacrifices of the Brahmins, as well as hunting and war. A practical result of this appears in one of the edicts of Aśoka, which forbids the killing and sacrificing of animals. The extension of kindness to animals was undoubtedly influenced by the doctrine of transmigration. Its far-reaching application of the principle made Buddhism the most tolerant of religions, for it has never extended itself by the sword or by force. But this very toleration was disastrous to it, especially when it came into contact with Islām. This commandment is only a wide extension of the principle of *ahiṃsā* which is also recognized in Hinduism. 'Thou shalt not kill' is also one of the ten Jewish commandments, but its scope there does not extend beyond the human race.

(*iii*) 2. 'Thou shalt not steal' is the second commandment. It means that one should refrain not only from taking what is not given, but from causing or approving of such action. On its positive side, it implies liberality. This prohibition is also identical with one of the Old Testament commandments.

(*iv*) 3. The third commandment is: 'Thou shalt not be unchaste.' It has a twofold application: with regard to laymen it prohibits adultery, but with regard to the monastic order it further enjoins celibacy. It is identical with the Hebrew commandment 'Thou shalt not commit adultery,' except that the latter does not imply celibacy, as in the Buddhist order.

(*v*) 4. The fourth commandment is: 'Thou shalt not lie.' The full meaning of this is, that falsehood of every kind, including calumny, misrepresentation, and false witness, is prohibited. It implies on the positive side that one should say only what is good of one's neighbour, not only what is conducive to harmony. It is partially identical with, though wider in its scope than, one of the ten Hebrew commandments: 'Thou shalt not bear false witness against thy neighbour.'

(*vi*) 5. The last of the five commandments is: 'Thou shalt not drink intoxicating liquors.' This also implies that one should not cause others to drink or approve of their doing so, because it leads to folly and ends in madness.

There is no corresponding prohibition among the commandments of the Hebrew Scriptures. It is a pity that this should be so, for as these commandments have been incorporated in Christian morality, the virtue of temperance would doubtless otherwise not be in such a backward state in the northern and western countries of Europe. The United States of America, apparently dissatisfied with the slow progress of temperance, have recently prohibited the sale of intoxicating liquors by law, but seemingly as yet without very conspicuous success. It is not quite clear how this law came to be passed: perhaps because every voter thought that it would be better for the country if his neighbour were forced to be sober, though not himself a believer in total abstinence, voting somewhat in the spirit of the Roman who said: 'I recognize the better course and approve of it, but I follow the worse.'

These five commandments are to be observed by the monk as well as by the layman; but there are five additional ones that are specially applicable to him. These enjoin that he should (6) not eat at unlawful times; (7) not engage in dancing, singing, music, or plays; (8) not use garlands, perfumes and ornaments; (9) not sleep in a high or broad bed; (10) not accept gifts of silver or gold.

(*vii*) The seventh stage of the eightfold path is right thought. This could only be represented by hymns in praise of Buddha and the church. There was no god to whom prayer could be addressed, and Buddha was only a human being who, after he had entered *parinirvāṇa*, no longer existed. Thus to the early phase of Buddhism prayer was unknown. Confessional formulas also find a place in the stage of right thought. The work called *Patimokha* (Sanskrit, *Pratimokṣa*) was a formulary of confession constituting one of the oldest parts of the Pāli canon. It is a list of sins enjoined by Buddha to be recited twice a month on the days of full and new moon in an assembly of at least four monks. At the end of each section the reciter inquired whether any of those present had transgressed any of the articles that it contained. These two confessional days are called *upavasatha* (Pāli, *uposatha*), a term originally meaning 'fast-day,' inherited from Brahmanism. The eighth day after new and the eighth day after full moon were also *upavasatha* days, though not for confession. These four days together constituted weekly recurring festivals of the nature of Sabbaths.

(*viii*) The eighth stage was right meditation. This takes the place of prayer in early Buddhism. Four stages are distinguished in this and can only be practised by monks. As aids to mental concentration exercises in expiration and inspiration were much indulged in. Thus, though Buddha rejected all self-mortification, he was not unsympathetic towards some of the practices of Yoga.

Throughout the system of Buddhist morality the personality of Buddha is prominent, and associated with it is esteem for individual liberty (as contrasted with rigid obedience to impersonal law), or at least for the spirit of liberation and liberalism. Though Buddha gave many precepts both in the theoretical and the practical sphere, they are expected to be followed not in the letter, but in the spirit. This comes out very clearly in Buddha's last sermon when he was about to enter into the Great Decease (*parinibbāṇa*). In this he urged that his disciples should leave off minor precepts and be themselves their own light. The value of this admonition cannot be over-estimated, when we note how it was handed on even in that school of Buddhists (*theravādins*) who were strict advocates of precedent. This liberal spirit is closely connected with the esteem shown for the **middle path** which is expressly stated in the very opening of Buddha's first sermon at Benares to be a fundamental principle of Buddhist ethics and remained its guiding spirit throughout the vicissitudes of its history. The middle path is recommended not merely because it lies in the middle between worldly pleasure and ascetic self-tortures, but because therein lies the right way for realizing the ideal in accordance with truth. It is this liberal and moderate spirit which distinguishes Buddhism from other ascetic orders, especially from the Jains; and it is owing to this spirit that, while Jainism remained to the last a formal asceticism, Buddhism was able, in its development, to adapt itself to the needs of various times and peoples. This was the main reason why Buddhism became a great world-religion, which neither Hinduism nor Jainism, owing to the rigidity of these systems, could ever have become. You will observe that the following of the middle path, an essential element in Buddhist morality, is practically identical with the Doctrine of the mean in Confucianism, as well as with the principle of moderation which we shall in a later lecture meet as the guiding spirit of Greek morality.

The full realization of the eightfold path and the attainment of enlightenment (*bodhi*) are necessarily associated with the final eradication of fundamental vice. This condition is expressed in the status of an *arhat* (Pāli, *arahat*) or 'saint,' who is free from all sins and desires, and, enjoying perfect mental calm, has attained earthly *Nirvāṇa*. Every Buddhist should aim at the attainment of saintship, and the only standard of this attainment is to be found in the personality of Buddha who is one of the *arhats*. In this respect the ideal of Buddhist morality consists in the imitation of Buddha (as is the imitation of Jesus in Christianity): this is the reason why faith in the master is so strongly insisted on for both moral and intellectual perfection. The ideal *arhat* sees in self-culture the first requisite of morality. This was the ideal of a section of conservative Buddhists who adhered rather to the letter than the spirit of the fundamental teaching. Opposed to this stream arose a more broad-minded school, which emphasized the importance of following Buddha's footsteps in spirit. This difference resulted in the division of the Hīnayāna and the Mahāyāna. In the former the ideal is the *arhat*, the self-centred saint, to whom self-culture is the first requisite of morality. To the Mahāyānist the ideal is the *bodhisattva*, who insists on the necessity of altruistic actions and thoughts, even for the sake of self-culture, as in the case of Buddha's former lives: the Bodhisattva is the teacher and benefactor of all beings. The Mahāyāna works for the sake of others in order to lead them to enlightenment. This system makes it possible for all beings to help each other on the way to salvation. In fact, this view is an altruistic one, while the other is an egotistical one. The Mahāyāna ideal from the moral point of view shows a highly important advance from a self-regarding to an other-regarding outlook. The practical results of this ideal were momentous. It may be said that Buddhist influence in China and Japan turned on this pivot, although it was accompanied with abuses as well.

The classification of the virtues as well as the vices, in Buddhist morality, consists of many enumerations, in which cross-divisions are not infrequent. As it would be both tedious and useless to discuss all these here, I will only mention what seems of importance.

The vices have in the first place to be guarded against and uprooted. The radical vice of human nature consists in egoism, which manifests itself in the three cardinal vices of lust (*kāma*), desire (*chanda*) and intention (*adhippaya*). These again manifest themselves in various forms, among which are included the so-called 'fetters' or incentives, one group of which consists of no fewer than one hundred and eight. Compared with the vices enumerated in the New Testament, which are thoroughly practical, these Buddhist classifications are more of the nature of psychological analysis of a hair-splitting order.

The virtues and virtuous practices are classified in seven groups, in all of which are included *faith, contemplation, and wisdom*, the three cardinal virtues of Buddhism, as being the essential basis before the other-regarding virtue of love can be applied in practical morality. In all the classifications, mental training plays a great part. Buddhism in fact lays more emphasis on the intellectual side than is done in Christianity. In this respect the Buddhist virtues may be compared rather with the Greek and the Confucian virtues: in the latter the cardinal virtues are *wisdom, love, and courage*. Faith, however, plays the central part as it does in Christianity.

The virtues which lead to perfection or the other shore (*pāram*) of Nirvāṇa are called *pāram-itās*: for the aim of

Buddhist morality is to bring men to the attainment of saintship or Buddhahood, the final goal of perfect enlightenment. Strictly speaking every virtue is a *pāramitā*; but in the Pāli books the term is applied exclusively to the moral acts of Buddha during his innumerable lives in preparation for his Buddhahood. Ten *pāramitās* are enumerated: they include charity (*dāna*), truthfulness (*sacca*), and love or charity in St. Paul's sense (*metta*). With these may be compared the ten *dharmas* in Manu requisite for attaining the highest resort (*paramaṃ gatim*). The *pāramitās* play a great part in the ethical system of the Mahāyāna, which brings them within the scope of all Buddhists, who must strive for perfect enlightenment. The *Saddharma-puṇḍarīka*, 'the lotus of the true law,' summarises these virtues. In the case of the Bodhisattvas, more consideration is paid to those among their virtues that have regard to others, and the essence of love is more prominent than in the ordinary treatment of the *pāramitās*.

The organization for the realization of the virtues and the promotion of morality was established in the Buddhist Order or *sangha*, which included monks and laymen. The guidance of morality therein was laid down by Buddha in the rules of obedience (*vinaya*), which included prohibitions and commandments, as well as the necessary measures of discipline for carrying them out. Though the vow of taking refuge (*saraṇa*) in the three jewels (*Buddha, dharma, sangha*), and the promise to keep the first five commandments in the ceremony of admission are common to all members of the order, a clear line of demarcation is drawn between the lay and the monastic disciples in regard to the other standards of life. Buddhism thus teaches a two-fold standard of morality: one, that of monks and nuns, which is beyond the world (*lokuttara*), and the other, that of the laity, which is worldly. A detailed description of worldly morality is given in the sermon to Singalaka: here the practice of filial piety, harmony between husband and wife, respect towards teachers, etc., are recommended as the deeds that shall bear good fruit in one's being born in heavenly worlds. But to be perfectly moral according to the Buddhist ideal, all the conditions of the *sīla* or moral code should be fulfilled; for this, the monastic or homeless life is a necessary condition. It is evident that Buddha recommended the life of an ascetic (*samana*) as the fittest for perfect morality, but at the same time did not exclude household life (*sagara*) entirely from salvation. The Buddhist community or Order (*sangha*) is made up of four classes of members: monks and nuns, laymen and lay-women. These four are always described as constituting one body and as equally praiseworthy when they are well disciplined. Moreover, we hear of a Brahmin named Vacchagotta, who praised the laws of Buddha because of their universal application to all his followers without distinction of conditions of life. Buddha himself is credited with having gone so far as to say that no difference existed between a layman and a monk, when they had realized a condition of perfect purity. We find several laymen and laywomen described as having attained saintship (*arhat*-ship), and it is evident that where there are differences of degree in their attainment, this is due to the difference in their state of emancipation from the fetters, and not to their respective conditions of life. Not a few lay disciples (*upāsakas*) are said to have cast off the five fetters and to have entered into perfect *parinibbāṇa* equally with many monks (*bhikkhus*). It is evident that many Upāsakas were in no way inferior to monks in moral perfection, and that Buddha allowed them the same honour as the monks. We may, in fact, safely conclude that Buddha did not make a fundamental distinction between these two classes of his disciples in regard to the degree of their moral and spiritual perfection. It is at the same time very evident that many could attain the moral ideal of Buddhism with less difficulty by means of the homeless than of the household life, on the same ground as St. Paul recommended celibacy to the followers of Christ. Hence the pre-eminently monastic character of Buddhist morality, and hence the duty of the lay members to show special respect to the monks.

Something similar can be said about the Buddhist view of the relation of the sexes. Generally speaking women are regarded as less capable of perfect morality because of their natural weakness and defects. Hence female ascetics or nuns (*bhikkhunīs*) are required to show special respect to the monks. Buddha himself was never tired of describing the defects and vices of women and of warning monks to guard against them. But this must not be ascribed simply to contempt for women, because similar warnings are given to women in regard to the wickedness of men. We know, too, how many excellent women played their part among Buddha's disciples.

With regard to lay life and the female sex it is to be noted that the Mahāyāna school took a higher view as a consequence of their Bodhisattava ethics. They take the former lives of Śākyamuni (Buddha) as the models of morality, which should at the same time be everyone's preparation for Buddhahood: hence they find the life of nobles or householders in no way incompatible with the practice of the *pāramitās* and the attainment of *bodhi* (enlightenment). In the Gandhāra sculptures we find the Bodhisattva Maitreya (the next Buddha) represented with garlands and other decorations, exactly like the figures of princes to be seen in the Barhut and Sānchī sculptures. Nearly every Mahāyāna book contains laudations of various Bodhisattvas and lay saints. Thus Vimalakīrti, a contemporary of Buddha, at Vaisāli, who lived the life of a rich man, dressed in fine clothes, driving in a smart carriage, and so on, at the same time aimed at the perfect practice of the *pāramitās* in the worldly life: his moral attainments were highly praised by Buddha; he is consequently regarded as a model Upāsaka among the Buddhists of the Far East even at the present day. Again Śrīmala, daughter of King Prasenajit, was deeply versed in Buddhist wisdom and perfect in her moral practice on the path of the Bodhisattvas. The great vows which she took in the presence of Buddha, and the dialogues between her and Buddha show that lay morality when associated with true wisdom, was able to take up the essence of all the rules enjoined upon monks and nuns and to elevate and broaden them to the all-embracing morality of the Mahāyāna. For the Mahāyānist, in short, the moral ideal consists in practising all the precepts of morality, regardless of the circumstances and conditions of life. A Mahāyāna text entitled *Brahmajāla* enumerates all Buddhist virtues and moral precepts, explaining them in higher senses, and according to the spirit of the Mahāyāna. It has become the standard of Buddhist Vinaya in China and Japan, and has exercised great influence upon the morality of both nations.

The authority by which the rules and precepts were carried out was the Sangha, the religious community as an ecclesiastical organization for the realization of the ideals aimed at, instituted by Buddha. It is, in fact, the Buddhist Church. Buddha was during his lifetime the sole authority on and leader of morality. After his death, a kind of apostolic succession, though not unified as claimed by the Christian Church, was kept up by a series of ordaining teachers (*upādhyāya* in Sanskrit), and every Buddhist could trace the lineage of his ordination through the series of teachers up to Buddha. This practice of receiving the precepts from an *upajjhaya* was observed both by monks and laymen even in Buddha's time, and parallel with this a kind of diocese was inaugurated and is continued to the present day. It is called the *sīma* (Skt. *sīman*), or the circle within which the wandering monks and nuns, as well as resident laymen, had to attend regular meetings and ceremonies conducted by the elders during the rainy seasons.

The personality of Buddha gave unity to the Order or Sangha. But he neither designated nor made provision for a successor as visible head of the Church. This necessarily resulted in the formation of many sects, of which two centuries after Buddha's death there were no fewer than eighteen with their own monasteries. There were 'elders' *thera*, (Skt. *sthavira*), in the Church, but they were not official, the term being merely an honorary title bestowed on monks who had long been ordained. The organization in the Buddhist Church was thus very loose and was undoubtedly a great cause of weakness throughout its history, and was one of the main causes leading to its ultimate downfall in India. Even in Buddha's own day his influence could not have extended over the many small and remote communities which were scattered all over India and beyond its confines owing to the great stress he laid on the propagation of his doctrine by means of missionaries.

Buddha himself is described in enthusiastic terms. It is said that no being, no Brahmin, no god can equal him, and no one can fathom his grandeur. Among his innumerable qualities thirty-two were later singled out as the characteristics of a great man. One of these, the *uṣṇīṣa*, a round excrescence on the top of the head, is always represented in the images of Buddha. In these there also generally appears between the brows a kind of wart (*ūrṇā*, Pāli, *unna*) which is described as emitting powerfully illuminating rays of light. Nevertheless Buddha was regarded as a man, perfect indeed, but mortal.

In the early days of Buddhism there was no worship in the form of prayers or sacrifice, because there was no god to whom they could be offered. But the worship of relics and the adoration of sacred sites soon began to develop. After the cremation of Buddha, his relics were divided into eight parts over which the various recipients built *stūpas*. The veneration of relics later became a much developed cult. With the rise of the Mahāyāna school representations of Buddha and of numerous Bodhisattvas suddenly appear in the

Buddhist monasteries in the region of Gandhāra in the extreme north-west of India, during the first century of our era. In this corner of India was created the conventional type of Buddha, which, spreading from here to other parts of India, was finally diffused over the whole of the Buddhist world. This type was probably created by some nameless Greek artist in the first century B. C. It has perhaps been the most enduring as well as the most widely dispersed type that the history of art has ever recorded. This figure furnishes melancholy evidence of the most striking feature in the degeneration of Indian Buddhism: Buddha, who denied the existence of a supreme god and rejected the worship of gods altogether, himself came to be treated as a supreme god, and the images representing him gave rise to a vast development of idolatry in the later forms of Buddhism.

In concluding this lecture, it will, I think, be useful to summarize the morality of Buddhism as showing a distinct advance in the direction of the service of man.

(A) Its general character was coloured by the goal Buddha had in view, *i.e.*, Nirvāṇa, attainable only by the destruction of desire: hence emphasis was laid on asceticism (excluding self-mortification as contrary to the doctrine of the Middle path).

On the religious side there was an absence of worship (prayer and sacrifice); the only religious feature being faith in Buddha and incipient veneration of sacred sites and relics.

(B) As regards the individual, emphasis was laid on self-culture, which was self-regarding in the Hīnayāna, while in the Mahāyāna it advanced to be other-regarding also. Social morality shows an advance from the customary to the conscious type, being regarded as of value only when based on wisdom (*prajñā*) and mental training (*samādhi* or *citta*). It also shows a social advance in the direction of altruism as based on love of one's fellow man (*maitri*). The advance from an egoistic to an altruistic stage is illustrated by the Hīnayāna ideal of the Arhat giving way to the Mahāyāna ideal of the Bodhisattva.

Lastly, Buddhism was the first religion to overstep the boundaries of nationality, and extend morality to its widest sphere, mankind, by means of missionaries sent to foreign countries. It was thus characteristically ascetic, moderate, altruistic, cosmopolitan.

Selected Bibliography.

H. Kern, *Manual of Indian Buddhism*, Strassburg, 1896; H. Oldenberg, *Buddha*, Berlin, 1903 (6th ed.); T. W. Rhys Davids, *Buddhism*, New York, 1907; M. Winternitz, *Geschichte der indischen Litteratur*, vol. ii, part 1, Leipzig, 1913.

LECTURE V

Greek Religion and Morality

We now come to the religion of another branch of the Aryan race, which existed in Eastern Europe from pre-historic times till it was supplanted by Christianity more than 1,500 years ago. I mean the religion of the Greeks. It cannot be passed over here because of its great importance both as having in its latest phase prepared the way for Christianity, and as having been the religion of the most gifted people of antiquity, that to which Europe owes the greater part of its intellectual inheritance. To Greece we owe the love of science, the love of art, the love of freedom, not one of these by itself, but all three combined in organic union. The Greek genius is the European genius in its first and brightest bloom. From contact with the Greek spirit arose that new and mighty impulse which we call progress. The Greeks above any other people of antiquity, possessed the love of knowledge for its own sake. Among them was born the idea that became the starting point of modern science, the idea that Nature works by fixed laws. By about 450 B. C. the general conception of law in the physical world was firmly established. It was the Greeks who discovered the sovereign efficacy of reason which in the pursuit of knowledge they applied clearly and fearlessly to every domain of life. This was connected with the awakening of the lay spirit. In the East the priests had generally held the keys of knowledge. But in Greece from the earliest times the sacerdotal influence was slight. Priests of course existed, but they never became a corporation, much less a caste. Typical of the Greek spirit is what the poet Euripides wrote: 'happy is he who has learned to search into causes, who discerns the deathless and ageless order of nature, whence it arose, the how and the why.'

In history—the Greek name for which, *historia* means 'search after truth'—the Greeks were the first who combined science and art, reason and imagination. The Chinese too produced history consisting of dry, prosaic chronicles. But the Greeks discovered another kind, in which reason and beauty were reconciled, one which the Romans borrowed, and which has served as a pattern to modern times. Thucydides in the 5th century B.C. is the best example of this.

The religion of a nation like this deserves examining as to whether it shows any progress in the direction of the service of humanity. Being an Aryan religion and historically known to us from about 900 B.C., not much later than the end of the Rigvedic period, and not altered by the modifications of any reformer like Zoroaster, it represents a natural development from the proto-Aryan age, just as the Vedic religion does. We must therefore expect it to have a very similar character. Unlike the Vedic religion, however, it was not handed down in the form of sacred books, but as almost entirely secular literature. Nevertheless this literature is deeply infused or preoccupied with religion and religious myth. There is thus plenty of material for the history of the Greek religion. It begins with the Epic poetry of Homer in the 10th or 9th century B.C., followed in the 8th and 7th by the poems of Hesiod and the so-called Homeric hymns; then comes the Lyric poetry of a religious character and the sententious-ethical-political poetry of the 5th century; next the tragic dramas, the greatest product of the poetical genius of Greece, and at the same time the great prose writers, the philosophers, historians and orators of the 5th century; among these is Herodotus the father of history, the intellectual ancestor of the modern anthropologist and student of comparative religion. In fact all the great fields of Greek literature have contributed information on the subject of religion. Among latter writers Plutarch and Pausanias (180 A.D.) have left valuable works, and the early Christian Fathers furnish us with a good deal of knowledge, though their evidence is somewhat biassed. Another and important source of the history of Greek religion is the monuments of art. For the high art of Greece was mainly religious, the greatest artists working for the religious service of the state.

The history of Greek religion may be divided into three periods: (1) 900-500 B.C., beginning with the Homeric poems and the colonial expansion of Greece, and ending before the Persian invasion; (2) 500-338 B.C., including the greatest century of Greek history, and closing with the battle of Chaeronea and the establishment of Macedonian supremacy; (3) the Hellenistic and Graeco-Roman period. The evidence of Greek inscriptions begins, *c.* 700 B.C., about 450 years before the oldest Aśoka inscriptions.

What information do the Homeric poems supply as to the state of Greek religion about 900 B.C.? We here find an advanced polytheism, a system in which the deities are already arranged in some sort of hierarchy, organized as a divine family under a supreme god. They are not vague and indefinite beings, though personal, like the Vedic gods; they are rather concrete and individual deities of robust and sharply defined personality; not spirits, but immortal beings of superhuman body and soul, conceived as glorified men. The Vedic gods represent an earlier phase: they would be at a similar stage, if they were all as fully personified and individualized as Indra, and if they were organized as a group under the rule of a single supreme god like Varuṇa. It is only exceptionally that some of the lower-grade deities like the river-gods, are not regarded anthropomorphically. The highest among them are not imagined as nature powers bound up with or inherent in the forces and departments of the natural world. Such a description applies only to wind-gods, and to the nymphs and gods of river and sea: also, though more loosely, to Helios (the Vedic Sūrya), the god of the sun. It scarcely applies to Poseidon, though his province is the sea; the 'rosy-fingered morn' is perhaps no more than a poetical personification (the corresponding Vedic 'radiant dawn,' Usas, is not much more). In fact Homer's typical god is a fully developed anthropomorphic being unconnected with any department of nature. Apollo, Hera, Athena, Hermes, and others show no sign that these divinities were conceived as nature-powers or as evolved from any part of the natural world. The high god Zeus (the Vedic Dyaus) though specially responsible for the atmospheric and celestial phenomena, is not identified with thunder or even with the sky, though a few phrases may reveal the influence of an earlier animistic conception of the divine Sky. The Greek and the Vedic conceptions of the same god Dyaus are typical of the degree of anthropomorphism in the two religions.

The religious tone in Homer, in many important respects represents an advanced morality. The god, though jealous and revengeful of wrongs or slights to himself, is on the whole on the side of righteousness and mercy; his displeasure is aroused by those who spurn the voice of prayer, who injure the suppliant, the guest, or even the beggar. Much of the religious reflexion in the epic poem is of an advanced type; thus Zeus at the beginning of the Odyssey declares that it is not the gods who bring evil to men, but that it is the wickedness of their own hearts that is the cause of all their ills.

The Homeric ritual is also on a higher level of theism. It shows no trace of savagery, and little contamination of religion with magic. The sacrifice is more than a mere bribe: it is a friendly communion with the god; and the service is solemn and beautiful with hymn and dance. The cult is furnished with altar and occasionally with temple and priesthood, but not yet, as a rule, with the idol, though this is beginning to appear. There was an altar in the courtyard of the house, around which kinsmen gathered and Zeus *herkeios* the god of the garth, was worshipped. Another sacred centre of the family life was the hearth and the hearthstone in the middle of the hall, and its sanctity is alluded to in the Homeric poems.

The ritual of the altar consisted in offering to the deity an animal victim or a gift of fruits and cereals. The sacrifice might be accompanied with wine or be wineless. The animal sacrifice seems to have represented a simple tribal or family communion-meal with the deity, whereby the sense of comradeship and clan-feeling between man and god was strengthened and nourished. There is insufficient evidence to prove that ancestor-worship existed in Homer's time, but it seems probable not only owing to its existence later, but because an early stage of it, as we have seen, is to be found among primitive men. But it seems certain that human sacrifice existed as an immemorial and enduring tradition of the race, and lingered here and there till the end of paganism.

At the beginning of this period is to be noted the rise of idolatry, when the image began in actual worship to take the place of the fetishistic object that represents an earlier stage. Idolatry gradually became almost universal, exercising a mighty influence on the religious sentiment of the Greeks, both before and after the triumph of Christianity. It intensified the already powerful instinct of polytheism, as it brought to the people a strong conviction of the real presence of the concrete individual divinity. It took deep root among the Greeks, because it was the greatest art in the world which evolved the ideal of divinity as based on the ideal of humanity. On the other hand, it was a form of worship that counteracted the development of a more spiritual religion, or of a divinity as an all-pervading spirit.

In secular life, the Homeric age had reached the higher agricultural stage. The basis of society was the family, founded on monogamy. The expansion of the civic system in this period, due to extended colonization and commerce, brought about a development of law and an expansion of moral and religious ideas. One of the most vital results of the institution of the *polis* or city was the widening of the idea of kinship. For in theory the city was a congregation of kinsmen, a combination of tribes, phrātries, and families wider or narrower associations, framed on a kin-basis; thus it gradually evolved the belief, leading to legal and moral development, that every citizen was of kin to every other.

As a result of the conception that the state was an extended family, certain ancient family cults were taken over by the religion of the city. As the private family had its centre in the hearth in the hall and the altar in the courtyard, so the city had its common Holy Hearth, upon which often a perpetual fire was maintained in its common hall; and the cult of Zeus was established in ancient days on the Akropolis of Athens. The great divinities of the State, Zeus, Hera, Aphrodite and Demeter, consecrated and regulated the monogamic rite of marriage, in which the city was directly interested. The city thus became and remained the Greek political unit based on kinship.

Another aspect of public life which gathered strength in this period was the custom of worshipping the hero or the mortal ancestor of the state. The earliest evidence we have of this custom dates from about 700 B.C. But there is reason, as I have indicated, for believing that the practice of heroizing the dead came down from the pre-Homeric age. It became of importance for the religious thought of the world, as encouraging the belief that human beings might through exceptional merit be exalted after death to a condition of blessed immortality, not as mere spirits, but as beings with glorified body and soul. A great stimulus was given to this practice by the expansion of Greek colonization, the greatest world-event of the period. A new hero-cult had to be instituted so as to bind the new citizens together by the tie of heroic kinship. The founder or leader of the new colony would naturally be selected for this honour, and his tomb would become a new centre to be visited yearly with annual offerings.

The close association of the city religion with the idea of kinship afforded a keen stimulus to local patriotism and would quicken an ardent life within the walls of the city. It had at the same time the defects of narrowness of view. But the old Greek idea of the god as father of the tribe or city contained the germ of the larger idea of God the Father of mankind, an idea which had already dawned on Homer at a time when the tribal spirit of religion was still at its height.

Another result of this system was that the state divinities became also the patrons and guardians of the family morality. Thus Zeus and Hera were the supervisors of human marriage and of the duties of married life. To marry healthfully and early, to beget strong children as defenders of the state and of the family graves, to cherish and honour parents, to protect the orphan: all these were patriotic religious duties inspired by the developed state religion and strenuously preached by the best ethical teachers of Greece.

From the earliest period of Greece the shedding of a kinsman's blood was a grave sin, while the slaying of one outside the kindred circle was ordinarily neither a sin against god nor a social crime. But with the growth of the kinship idea based on the unity of the city or *polis*, the crime began to be dealt with by the state and not by the clan of the slain man. Thus gradually a civilized law of homicide grew up, and by the 7th century B.C. any Greek state could legally establish the difference between the act of murder and the act of justifiable or accidental homicide.

From about 700 B.C. the oracle of the god Apollo at Delphi became the chief centre and the strongest bond of spiritual unity in the Greek world. When the Greek race was rapidly establishing that chain of colonies across and around the Mediterranean which were to spread Greek culture throughout the world, it became the fashion to consult the Delphic Apollo as to the choice of the site. To political unity it could not contribute much owing to the disruptive tendency of Greek politics which could not get beyond the idea of the city state as the national unit; but the influence of the Delphic oracle at any rate contained within it the germs of intertribal morality and concord.

In the sphere of religion it did not go much beyond emphasizing the necessity of purification from bloodshed. In the sphere of morality its standard was generally high and its influence beneficial, especially in the later period when its utterances reflected the progress of Greek ethics, and the spirit of an enlightened humanitarianism. But its chief religious achievement was to introduce some principle of order into the complex aggregate of Greek polytheism and to deepen the impression on the Greek mind of the divine regulation of the world. The results of this influence of the Delphic oracle we can trace in the works of Athenian tragedy and in the history of Herodotus. It may seem somewhat strange that the Delphic priesthood never attempted to impose Apollo as the supreme god on the Greek states. But he never appears as more than the minister of Zeus, the mouthpiece of the Father-god, the tradition of whose supreme position among the Aryan Greeks had been too firmly established by Homer and his school.

It may at first seem surprising that games should have had any religious significance. Yet it is a fact. The great Hellenic games, which began to arise and develop early in this period, were always connected with the worship of gods or heroes. These games must be regarded as one of the strongest

Pan-Hellenic influences arousing and strengthening the feeling of nationality. In the 6th century B. C. the whole of Greece, eastern and western, was represented at Olympia. At Olympia, once in every four years, the Pan-Hellenes offered a common homage to their ancient Father-god, the Olympian Zeus. The Delphic Oracle and the great Games, then, were very important elements in the religious national life, as tending to develop a broader type of religion. The games also influenced the higher mental history of the Greek race generally, because most of them included competitions in art and literature.

Another religious influence of great moment in the spiritual history of Greece is the spread of the worship of Dionysos. Its chief effect on the polytheism of Greece was its stimulation of a stronger religious faith. Later it had the special effect on the popular religion of refining and brightening men's beliefs about the life after death and the powers of the lower world. Its highest importance, however, lay rather in the esoteric than in the popular sphere of Greek religion. By *c.* 600 B.C. the cult of Dionysos was promoted by the rise and spread of what are called the Orphic brotherhoods who worshipped this god under various mystic names. The preachers of the Orphic doctrines are the first propagandists or missionaries that we can trace in the pre-Christian Mediterranean world. Having a definite message, and, ignoring the tribal and city barriers of the old political religion, they preached their message, if not to all mankind, at least to all the Greeks. They proclaimed a theory, unfamiliar to native Greek mythology and religion, that the soul of man is divine and of divine origin. Engrossed with the problem of life after death, the Orphic mystics evolved the notion of purgatory, a mode of punishment after death which is temporary and purificatory ; possibly also the dogma of reincarnation or of a cycle of lives both in this world and the next. This latter idea has suggested to students of religious philosophy that

Indian speculation may have affected the west as early as the 6th century B.C. The part played by these preachers of purity and salvation in the later spiritual history of Greece was of great importance. Another kind of mysteries were those of Eleusis. These were more national and Pan-Hellenic than the Orphic, but their influence and purpose were similar. By about 600 B.C. they already appealed to the whole Grecian world: their special promise to the initiated being the happiness of the soul after death. The only limit to admission to this brotherhood was the possession of Greek speech and purity from actual stain; the initiation being open to women and sometimes even to slaves. Its influence seems to have lasted till the introduction of Christianity (*c.* 300 A.D.). Their doctrines were the highest and most spiritual product of the pure Hellenic religion. While Pan-Hellenic, they belong to the sphere of personal religion; for they satisfied the craving of the individual for closer fellowship with the deity, and allayed the fears that were growing up in this period, as to the individual destiny. Thus by *c.* 500, the Greeks had become conscious of their national unity in intellectual culture, morality and religion. Zeus was no longer a tribal deity but had now become the god of all the Greeks.

The two most striking phenomena in the spiritual history of the 6th century were: (1) the rise and expansion of Ionian philosophy, and (2) the development of a new form of literature, the Athenian drama. Both of these were forces affecting the popular religion.

There were only two nations of antiquity that produced a philosophy of their own: the Greeks and the Indians. That of the Indians became a religious philosophy; that of the Greeks later became the source of the secular science of Europe. So far as the new Greek speculation dealt with the physical origin of things, it did not clash with any orthodox prejudice of the average Greek, for he had no sacred books that dictated to him what to believe about the origin of the world or the constitution of nature. Thus when Herakleitos said: 'neither god nor man made the world (*kosmos*),' there was no authoritative Greek myth or dogma to contradict him. But the great philosophers of the 6th century, Pythagoras, Empedocles, Xenophanes, and Herakleitos, were also directly concerned with the philosophy of religion such as speculations on the nature of the godhead. Some of their utterances were here in sharp conflict with the conceptions and ritual of the current polytheism. Thus their speculations tended to run counter to the anthropomorphic theory of divinity, for they tended to define god not as a person, but rather as the highest spiritual or metaphysical, or even physical power or function of the universe; but there is a common tendency away from the pantheistic view such as appears in the Brahma of the Upanishads. Xenophanes was the philosopher who uttered the most severe protests against the current religious conceptions of Greece. In particular he strongly attacked the folly of anthropomorphism, the dominating passion of Greek polytheism. It is clear that for him the godhead was only a cosmic principle. Herakleitos seems to have held similar views; in his surviving fragments he speaks with scorn about methods of purification from blood and the folly of idolatry. At first such protests could have influenced only a few; it was not till the 5th century that the state religion was obliged to take notice of them.

The second striking phenomenon of the 6th century was the Attic drama, the greatest of all the post-Homeric literary achievements of Greece; it was inspired by the cult of Dionysus.

II. The second period of Greek religion extends over not much more than a century and a half, from 500 B. C. to the downfall of the independence of the Greek states after the battle of Chaeronea (B. C. 338). It embraced the greatest period of not only Greek history, but of human history as a whole: it embraced the victory of Greece over the great Persian empire; the rise and fall of the Imperial City State; the culmination of the greatest plastic art in the world; the maturity of the Athenian drama; the diffusion of education and the spirit of enquiry through the sophists; and the higher development of philosophy and science.

If we compare Greek religion at the beginning of this period with that of the Homeric age, we find the same gods worshipped, including even rivers and streams; while some other animistic practices still existed. This religion was still a living faith, still untouched by the influence of science and philosophic scepticism. During the greater part of the fifth century polytheism was probably stronger even than it had ever been in the past. Its anthropomorphism is even more pronounced owing to the great development of art. There is however, a deeper conviction of the part played by moral agencies and powers in the affairs of men. Herodotus sets forth a religious view of history, of which there are only faint signs in the epics. He regards the mighty struggle between Greece and Persia as a conflict of moral forces, the result being worked out by unseen powers such as Nemesis (retribution), Violence and Justice, with Zeus acting as the righteous Judge. The successful struggle against the barbarians undoubtedly deepened the devotion to the national cults and the gods in whom they had trusted. These great events also gave a stimulus to hero-worship: some of those who fell in the great battles against the invader, received heroic honours. The heroizing of those who had recently died in the service of their country had its moral value as a strong incentive to patriotism. The general effect of the religious art of the 5th and early 4th century, which must be called the most perfect religious art of the world, had the effect of confirming the already existing idolatry. Greek polytheism would have perished far sooner than it did, if Greek art had not fortified and ennobled it.

The influence of the great poets of the 5th century on religion was also considerable. The great lyrist and ode-writer Pindar, and the two dramatists Aeschylus and Euripides, all three, with some freedom of criticism, accepted the existing religious order, desiring to ennoble, not to destroy it. All of them preach the supremacy of Zeus, his omnipotence and perfect justice, while Sophocles emphasizes his mercy.

To these poets Zeus is generally a definite personal Being. Once at least, however, Aeschylus, defines Zeus pantheistically: for he says 'Zeus is air, earth, heaven; Zeus is the whole of things, and whatever is higher still than these.' The poets, too, sometimes represent the gods as moral powers, not as concrete individual deities. These may then be called personifications of moral ideas, as, *e. g.*, in Aeschylus 'Justice, the maiden daughter of God.' The great 5th century poets are all moralists: we find them protesting against repulsive stories such as the cannibalism of the gods in the myth of Pelops, or against blasphemous stories about combats of heroes against divinities with the words: 'Let all war and strife stand far apart from the immortals.' But neither Pindar nor Aeschylus and Sophocles protest against the more licentious myths about the amours of the gods. In fact, the axiom that sexual purity was an essential attribute of all divinity was not yet accepted by the higher thought of Greece.

The two older dramatists, however, moralize, as far as possible, the legends with which they deal. Aeschylus also protests against the superstitious doctrine of Nemesis; he emphasizes moral responsibility and the moral continuity that links our lives and actions, while Sophocles displays a deep conviction of the eternity and divinity of the moral law.

Quite different was the position of the latest of the three great dramatists, Euripides. He must be regarded as the popularizer of the new enlightenment. He came under the influence of the paid sophist, the pioneer of modern education and the first champion of the critical spirit; he knew and associated with Socrates and the philosophers Protagoras and Anaxagoras, imbibing deeply their spirit and their teaching. He was a doubting believer in polytheism, nor can he be said to have believed in any part of it firmly. He is evidently animated by the new idea that vengeance is alien to the perfect nature of god: this was still more insisted upon by the Pythagoreans, by Plato, and later philosophers. Euripides' protest against divine licentiousness is based on his conviction that purity in every sense was essential to the divine nature. His leading principle in all these matters is expressed in one of his dramas, *viz.*, that the evil in religious practice and legend arises from men imputing their own evil nature to God. He was the first man who uttered this warning against a debasing anthropomorphism. His attitude reminds one of the cynical remark of, I think, Voltaire: 'God created man in his own image, and man lost no time in returning the compliment.' The stories about the gods were often of the type of savage folk-lore; and not being enshrined in sacred books that could speak with authority to the people (like the old Testament to the Hebrews), were less liable to arrest the growth of a higher ethical-religious spirit, than the influence of such books. Euripides seems to have had an antipathy to some divinities, especially Apollo and Aphrodite; but against the actual forms of Greek ritual and worship he had no special objection. He protests, however, against human sacrifice as a barbaric and non-Hellenic institution. He does not belittle the value of sacrifice in general; on the contrary he once says that the small sacrifice of the pious often outweighs a hecatomb (*i.e.*, the public sacrifice of 100 oxen).

Much in the sententious poetry of Euripides might have elevated the religious thought of his age; but the pantheistic tendency of his conception of the divine nature could hardly have been reconciled with the anthropomorphic polytheism of the people. In another respect Euripides showed a great advance in the moral direction, which, however, in the long run was to undermine the old city religion, *viz.*, his humanitarian or cosmopolitan instinct, which allowed him to sympathize with Trojans, women, children and slaves, and inspired him with the noble thought that 'the whole world is the good man's fatherland.'

As a result of such growing enlightenment, the religious view of human life and conduct was becoming more spiritual and inward. The doctrine begins to be proclaimed that god as a spiritual power can read the heart of man, and judges him by his thoughts; that sin lies not in the external act alone; that ritual purity is of less value than purity of soul. The spread of such thoughts in the 5th century, helped to mould the later religious history of Europe.

Among the thinkers who influenced the religious world most before the downfall of Greek independence was the philosopher Plato. He appeared not as a destroyer, but as a reformer; for his purpose was to purge mythology of its stories of divine conflicts, divine vengeance, divine amours. As these were not enshrined in sacred books, he felt that he could do this gently and easily without disturbing the recognized forms of worship. He did not desire to weaken the established religion. In fact he accepted some of its data, such as the belief in the nativity of the gods. In this case he concluded that gods who were born could not be essentially immortal; Zeus could thus not be accepted as the absolute and supreme ruler of the world-order (*kosmos*). Plato's system further sets forth the notion of an immortal element in man, which again agrees with the popular belief of the period in the survival of some part of our being after death.

The philosophy of Plato can in fact be shown to have influenced the later history both of pre-Christian and of Christian religious thought. We may with probability conclude that he greatly helped to spread the belief of the spiritual nature and perfection of God, to destroy the prevailing ideas of divine vindictiveness and jealousy, to explain the external world spiritually rather than materialistically, to accept the belief in the divine nature of the human soul, and in the importance of its life after death, as partly dependent on the attainment of purity.

III. The Third Period begins after the battle of Chaeronea in 338 B.C. The establishment of the Macedonian Empire naturally led to the decline of deities like Apollo of Delphi and Zeus and Athene, because of their political connexion with the state religion. But Greek polytheism was still able to win its way in other countries, as it captured Carthage in the fourth century, and in the third began to spread in Rome and the Roman Empire. But generally speaking personal religion was beginning to gain strength, and to arouse an individual craving for a more intimate union with the divinity. This craving was satisfied by private brotherhoods devoted to the special worship of one deity. Their religious importance was far-reaching. Thus they show the development of the idea of a humanitarian religion, as they generally overstepped the limits of the old tribal and city religion, by admitting strangers. The members here, both men and women, were drawn together by their personal devotion to a particular deity, to whom their relation was far more intimate and individual than that of the ordinary citizen could be to the gods of his tribe and city. Their organization too produced a deeper sense of religious fellowship between the members, and later became a model to the early Christian community.

But what is still more striking, they show that fusion of East and West which Alexander the Great, the man who opened the Gates of the East, and his successors aimed at producing. For many of these religious brotherhoods, whose members and organization were Greek, were devoted to foreign deities, such as Adonis, so that they unconsciously acted as missionaries in the great movement of blending Eastern and Western religions and divinities.

An important influenbe in the Greek religion of this period was that of the dramatist Menadder, the friend of Epicprus and the admirer of Euripides, the heir of the hhmanitarian spirit which had been developing in the century before Alexander's conquests in the East. There is no doubt that Menander was actually revered as an ethical religious teacher. He is the mouthpiece of cosmopolitanism in ethics and religion. Thus one of his sayings is: 'No good man is alien to me; the nature of all is one and the same.' Many of the fragments of Menander show strikingly close resemblances to the teaching of the New Testament, and are of essential importance for the history of Greek ethics. As to religion, we again find that he did not make a general attack on the popular polytheism, though he protested against superstition and the extravagance of sacrifice offered as a bribe. But many of his sayings indicated the development of a more personal, more inward, more spiritual religion than that ordinarily prevailing. God is presented as a spirit and as spiritually discerned by the mind of man. Here you have a passage that has survived from one of his unknown comedies: 'a guardian spirit stands by every man, straightway from his birth, to guide him into the mysteries of life, a good spirit; for one must not imagine that there is an evil spirit injuring good life, but that God is utterly good.' It is to be noted that this poet was very popular with a wide audience.

The tolerant humanitarianism of Menander is reflected in the theocrasia, or fusion of the divinities of East and West. It is apparent from Herodotus, how natural it was to the Greek mind to interpret the deities of foreign nations by its native pantheon; and it was easy for Euripides to commend the Phrygian Kybele as Demeter. We know that the Greeks who visited India with Alexander's army, identified several of the Indian gods with Greek divinities. Before Alexander's time, however, it was both difficult and even dangerous to introduce any unauthorised foreign cult into the city-state.

But after Alexander, it became the far-sighted policy of some of his successors to establish some common cult that might win the devotion of the Greek and Oriental peoples alike. This was the intention of Ptolemy, when he founded at Alexandria the cult of the Babylonian god Serapis, whom the Egyptians, owing to similarity of name, were able to identify with their Osiris-Apis. The name of Zeus was applied to so many gods of the East that it often seemed to have lost all its personal and concrete value and to have acquired the more general meaning of 'God.' Even the Jewish God Yahweh himself was thus occasionally identified with Zeus.

This blending movement was of the greatest importance for religious thought. The Christian writer Augustine records the view of the Roman Varro that the name of the deity made no difference so long as the same thing is understood, and that therefore the god of the Jews was the same as Jupiter. This is a great idea bequeathed to the world by Greek tolerance and Greek sanity. This expression of Greek enlightenment prepared the way for monotheism, and thus indirectly for Christianity. It could also encourage the pantheistic idea of a diffused omnipresent spirit of divinity, such as is expressed by Aratus, the scientific poet of the 3rd century B. C.

Such pantheistic speculation is to be found in some of the dogmas of Stoicism. For most of the Stoic thinkers divinity was less a personal concrete being than a spiritual force or soul-power immanent in things. Their system was, however, antipathetic to the social religion of the kin-group and of the city. Its founder Zeno is said to have protested against shrines and idols; but he did so in vain: Stoicism had no effect on the religion of the average man of the people.

The Cynic school of philosophy was the most aggressive against the popular creeds and cults, with its caustic and outspoken criticism; but it too had no appreciable effect. The Hellenistic religions are as convincedly theistic and idolatrous as the older were. The chief change in the period was that a man might now to some extent choose his own divinity, being no longer limited to the one into the worship of which he was born. This freedom had already for some time been offered by the brotherhoods; and now, especially through the powerful and wide influence of the cult of Asklepios, the god of medicine, the idea was developed of a deity who as Healer and Saviour called all mankind to himself. In a treatise called *Asklepios*, a long address and prayer to this deity are preserved, of which the tone is strikingly Christian.

Personal or individual religion was stimulated by the growth of certain non-Hellenic mysteries in the Mediterranean area during the later centuries of paganism, those of Attis and the great Mother, the Egyptian Isis, and in the last period, of Mithra. Many interesting ideas are to be found in these mysteries. Such are community with the deity through sacrament; the mystic death and rebirth of the convert preparing for baptism; the saving efficacy of baptism and purification. Most of these mystic societies also proclaimed the immortality of the soul, a happy resurrection, and a divine life after death. The mysteries of Mithra came to the Graeco-Roman world only in the latest period before the establishment of Christianity and gained little hold on Greek society proper. The most attractive mystery for the Greeks was the Orphic: it was active in the two centuries before and after the beginning of our era.

The idea of many of these mystic brotherhoods, that the mortal might achieve divinity, is illustrated by another religious phenomenon which stands out in this latest period, *viz.*, the worship of individual men and women, either in their lifetime or immediately after death.

We have seen that in the 6th and 5th centuries B. C. the Greek was willing to concede heroic honours to certain distinguished men after death. But divine worship being offered to a living person was a different thing. The most striking examples of deification of this kind are the kings of the

Seleucid and Ptolemaic dynasties, who usually enjoyed divine honours after death, and sometimes bore divine titles such as 'Saviour,' and 'God' in their lifetime. Such deification of a mortal, so prevalent in this later period, may be considered a moral and religious evil. It was, in any case, a momentous fact belonging to the history of European religion; for it familiarized the Graeco-Roman world with the idea of the incarnation of the Man-God.

Thus in this last period we can trace the decay of civic and political religion, especially of the cults of Apollo, Zeus and Athene; while a living, personal religion shows itself to be more diffused than in earlier centuries. The horizon of religion now lies beyond the grave, and its force is derived from the other world. Men flock to the mysteries seeking communion with the divinity by sacrament. The religious virtue now most emphasized is purity. The earlier morality looked to works and practice, the later to purity and faith. We now see the rise of a humanitarian spirit which was to inspire a new cosmopolitan religion.

A historical survey of Greek religion shows that it maintained itself at a higher level of polytheism for more than 1000 years, during which it made certain unique contributions to the evolution of society and the higher intellectual life of man. By the side of its higher aspects many of the products of lower and savage culture survived. These were mainly obliterated by Christianity. Many of them are found in all higher religions, usually in a moribund state. Anthropomorphism was the strongest bias of the Greek religious imagination, and with this is connected a passion for idolatry and hero-worship. These tendencies show a decided influence on Greek Christianity, and generally speaking modern research has tended to show that Christian dogma and ritual are much more indebted to the later Greek paganism than is usually supposed.

In what I have said up to this point I have traced the gradual elevation of Greek religion from the earliest historical times down to the rise of Christianity. I now propose to consider the advance of Greek morality, taken separately, from a narrow to a wider outlook. The popular view at the present day regarding the nature of morality is that it consists of an established code of precepts and obligations which have been framed to regulate human conduct, and that it rests ultimately upon a religious sanction. But as their religion, at least as far as the cult of the Olympian gods is concerned, did not include any such code, the Greeks in the early period hardly recognized any connexion between morality and religion. They had, it is true, a vague and misty belief that wrongdoers were punished after death, but this was not a doctrine that influenced the conscience of the ordinary man. The sinner was punished not as a moral offender, but as a trespasser against a vindictive power. The general attitude towards the conception of a future life was one of contemptuous indifference. Thus Achilles in the Odyssey says: 'rather would I be a serf on some poor man's farm than lord over all the spirits of the dead.' So little did the early Greek (any more than apparently the Vedic Indian) care to extend his vision to the other side of the grave.

Equally indefinite was the belief that wickedness is punished in this life. Such a view was so obviously opposed to the facts of everyday experience that the believer in divine justice was obliged to suppose that punishment is sometimes reserved for another generation, while the scoffer was convinced that the gods did not pay any regard to the affairs of man. There was thus a tendency to believe that true wisdom consisted in recognizing human impotence and counselling resignation to a lot which is inevitable. Hence the advice is again and again inculcated that man should acquiesce in destiny, bear misfortune with a stout heart, and as a mortal avoid arousing the jealousy of the gods.

If we inquire what the actual standard of morality was in the various stages of Greek history, we find that, in the earliest or Homeric age (about 900 B.C.), the exercise of the humaner virtues was restricted to the bounds of the family or clan; but there is evidence that within these limits morality was highly developed. Monogamy was the type of marriage, and women enjoyed greater freedom and influence than they did later at Athens. (Here again we have a parallel with the early period in India.) An elevated sense of honour is apparent. Hospitality is a well-established virtue, beggars and suppliants having an indefeasible claim to it. There is also evidence of the gentle treatment of horses and dogs. But behind these virtues there is a background of hardness and cruelty. In his wrath the Homeric hero was a savage. Thus when a town was captured old women and children were slain, and young women were carried off as the property of the victors.

Somewhat later than Homer, the poet Hesiod, in the 8th century, expresses the sentiments of a lower stratum of society. We find here the spirit of commercial prudence: the hardness of the struggle against poverty is emphasized, while the excessive importance attached to money is complained of. The virtues here recommended are temperance and simplicity, industry and fair dealing. Unjust judges who rob the poor are censured.

In the age of the sententious poetry of the 7th century B.C. (which resembles the much later Sanskrit type of the *Nītiśāstras*), thought began to be consciously directed to moral questions. Here the morality which was merely implicit in Homer receives separate treatment and distinct expression in the form of a mass of proverbial wisdom. We here find the maxims which had been collecting for centuries in the Greek mind condensed into a few pregnant sentences. The poets were the educators of Greece; and to this age belongs the formulation of all that was most characteristic in Greek popular poetry. The dramatists of the fifth century were steeped in this literature. From this period comes the famous saw 'nothing too much' attributed to Solon, and repeated by another sage in the form of 'measure (*i.e.*, moderation) is best.' This saying represents the innermost core of Greek sentiment, and may be said to be the keynote of the Greek character. Aristotle, the tutor of Alexander the Great, followed the popular opinion inherent in this maxim, when in the 4th century B.C. he defined virtue as a mean between extremes. He had, you remember, been anticipated in this by Confucius. The intellectual aspect of Greek morality appears best in the maxim *gnothi scauton* 'know thyself.' This saying and *mēden agan* constitute a very epitome of the Greek genius. A Greek writer (Ion) commenting on this maxim remarked: "'know thyself' is a short saying, yet it is a task so great that Zeus alone can master it."

Among these poets of the 7th century we find an increased recognition of the importance of justice, as might be expected from their national bias towards the mean. Here are a few of their utterances. Theognis says: 'dishonesty issues finally in ruin' (the equivalent expressed 2,500 years ago, of 'honesty is the best policy'). Another poet (Chilon) gives the advice: 'choose loss rather than shameful gain.' A third (Phocylides) went so far as to declare that all virtue is comprehended in justice. Such thoughts led the poets to comment on the slowness of the gods in punishing the unjust. They were forced to conclude that, while the actual sinner escaped, his crime was expiated by the sufferings of his descendants. They do not, however, protest against the injustice of the gods; the existence of the injustice never leads them to doubt the existence of the gods. They simply conclude that the ways of the gods are past finding out; and Theognis mournfully acquiesces in the punishment of the innocent for the sin of the guilty. But there was a limitation to the poets' conception of justice: it excluded any consideration for enemies. Thus one of them (Pittacus) says: 'Do not speak ill of your friend, or well of your enemy.' Deceit towards enemies was also considered justifiable. The dramatists had not advanced much beyond this last point of view. Thus Aeschylus acquiesced in righteous deception and the lie in season; Sophocles also declared that falsehood was justified if it brought final success. The standard of the philosopher Plato was much higher; for he observed: 'men are too fond of saying that at proper times falsehood may be justified'; he also anticipated Christian morality by combating the popular view and maintaining that the good man will not harm another.

In the second period (after 500 B.C.), the conventional morality of the poets and of the dramatists continued to be the standard at Athens. But Euripides, who praises Athens as the protector of the weak, advocates the generous treatment of a beaten foe, at a time when certain atrocities inconsistent with such principles took place; the true spirit of an age must, however, be gathered from the aspirations of its leading minds. The moral horizon of the Greeks was widening. The Pan-Hellenic spirit produced by the Persian wars was best represented by Pindar, who felt himself so little a member of a particular state that all Greece could feel proud of his genius. The Greeks had now arrived at a wider human outlook, the national one, and no longer occupied the tribal social standpoint. Aeschylus, the oldest of the tragic dramatists, took so deep an interest in the highest problems of morality, that he has often been compared to a Hebrew prophet. His leading motive was to find a moral lesson that could be traced through the horrors and cruelties of the old legends, and especially to discover how the interference of the gods in human affairs could be reconciled with the requirements of justice. Undoubtedly he was a loftier moralist than any of the earlier poets. We cannot conceive him as justifying a falsehood for the sake of obtaining a practical advantage. Thus he says: 'The mouth of Zeus knows not how to lie, and all his words he will fulfil.' He was especially concerned to find an answer to the old problem of divine justice, why the sins of the fathers are visited upon the children. Aeschylus in effect denies this doctrine as completely as the Hebrew prophet Ezechiel does in the Old Testament. He shows in the fate of Agamemnon that he was not punished for his father's sin, but for a new sin committed by himself; for there is always a new sin in such cases. As to the question, how sin first came to be committed, Aeschylus definitely rejected the traditional view which attributed it to the jealousy of the gods aroused by great prosperity.

We may then say that the dramatic poets both purified human morality and removed immoral traits from the character of the gods. The epoch of the great dramatists brings us to the class of professional educators who described themselves as 'teachers of virtue,' the sophists, the chief of whom was Socrates. The teaching of morality was henceforth to be considered as the proper function of philosophy. Here Plato must be regarded as having contributed most towards diffusing the belief in the moral perfection of the divine nature as well as towards purifying the conception of human morality.

In the last period (after 338 B. C.) we observe how the introduction after Alexander's time of theocrasy, by means of which different nationalities began to worship the same deity, broke down national barriers and encouraged international relations. At the same time, the dramatic poet Menander encouraged the diffusion of the humanitarian spirit and became the advocate of cosmopolitanism in the Grecian world.

In this connexion it is interesting to ask what was the general attitude of the Greeks to the non-Hellenic world? All other nations were to them Barbarians, but not quite in the same sense as was the case with other ancient peoples. To the Greeks 'know thyself' meant not only to know the Grecian man, but to know foreigners. To this study they were impelled not solely, or even chiefly, by a commercial and gain-seeking instinct, such as moved the Phoenicians, but by a single-hearted desire to know. Indians, Egyptians, Chinese did not care to penetrate beyond their own frontiers. But the Greeks were travellers. Of Odysseus Homer said: 'Many were the men whose towns he saw and whose mind he learnt.' In this he is typical of his race. We are often told that the Greeks were exclusive, and their phrase 'barbarian' for a foreigner looks a little contemptuous. But the invidious meaning was acquired only by degrees, and not perhaps without reason; in any case it is a less invidious term than 'devils' applied by many Easterns to their neighbours. It is at any rate significant that Aristotle thought it worth his while to analyze and describe the constitutions of a hundred and fifty-eight states, including in his survey not only Greek states but those of the barbarian world. This great Greek philosopher was the first student of what we call Comparative Politics. We see the same spirit apparent in the History of Herodotus more than a century earlier. Though he is describing the great conflict between the West and the East, the Greeks and the Barbarians, he had no hard words for the Barbarians. He can view them with candid surprise and impartiality. Here we have a real advance towards cosmopolitanism such as was found in no other ancient people.

To sum up: Greek religion appears as a developed anthropomorphic polytheism persisting from the earliest period for more than 1000 years, but showing some signs before the beginning of our era of possibly developing into monotheism. Greek morality, in the beginning limited to the sphere of the family and the kin-group, in the last period extended its horizon so as to include the whole human race.

Selected Bibliography.

L. R. Farnell, *Cults of the Greek States*, 5 vols., Oxford, 1896-1910; J. E. Harrison, Themis, *a Study of the Social*

Origins of Greek Religion, Cambridge, 1912; J. G. Frazer, *Attis, Adonis, Osiris*, London, 1907; Goblet d'Alviella, *Eleusinia*, Paris, 1903; P. Foucart, *Le Culte de Dionysos en Attique*, Paris, 1904; E. Caird, *Evolution of Theology in the Greek Philosophers*, 2 vols., Glasgow, 1904; J. Adam, *The Religious Teachers of Greece*, Edinburgh, 1908.

LECTURE VI

JUDAISM.

We now come to the surviving Semitic religions, which have exercised an enormous influence on the history of the world. There are three of them: Judaism, Muhammadanism, and Christianity. The first and much the oldest is Judaism, the parent of the other two, which have overspread the greater part of the globe.

Judaism is the religion of the Jews, otherwise called Hebrews or Israelites, the people that, though not homogeneous, became a single nation in Palestine, about 1000 years before Christ. Consisting of nomadic, pastoral tribes, this people about that time invaded from the South and occupied Palestine, the land of the Canaanites, which lies between Egypt and Mesopotamia, and the inhabitants of which were a cognate Semitic race. The size of this land in its widest extent is about 6,000 square miles or less than one-fifth of the area of England (excluding Wales and Scotland). The Jewish religion became a strictly monotheistic one, but remained a national (and not a universal) one, because the Jews regarded themselves as the chosen people of a particular god. Similarly, the god of Judaism is not a universal god of mankind, but a tribal or national god, the god of the Jews. It has, moreover, two characteristic negative features. the rejection of polytheism and of idolatry, features which its daughter religions have inherited. It differs from Christianity in rejecting any mediator between God and man, and from Zoroastrianism in rejecting any cosmic force of evil. Like Zoroastrianism it is a juristic religion, *i.e.*, one that requires the fulfilment of a code based on works (*karma-mārga*) rather than belief. It is a system of human conduct, a law of righteousness according to which a man should live. Thus one conforming to this law could find salvation, because the Jewish religion, in its later development, teaches that every righteous man, apart from his beliefs, has a share in the world to come.

The earliest ancestor of the Jewish people was traditionally held to have been Abraham whom they believed to have made with Jehovah, as his one and only God, a covenant of which the rite of circumcision was the symbol to hold good with his descendants as the chosen people of Yahweh. When the Jews entered Palestine, there was borne before them a chest or shrine, commonly called the Ark, which symbolized the presence of Yahweh, which probably contained the image representing Yahweh in the form of a brazen serpent, and the presence of which in battle was considered necessary to ensure victory. Thus Yahweh seems, in the earliest times, to have been regarded as a god of war.

Of the general character of the religion of the Israelite tribes at the time of the conquest of Palestine we possess no direct information. Having till then been nomads they probably lived mainly on milk, like the Todas of modern India, and practised sacrifice only to a limited extent, being unable to spare many animals from their flocks, on which their existence mainly depended. Though it is uncertain whether they already worshipped their national god Yahweh (usually called Jehovah by English-speaking people) under that name, there is evidence to show that they worshipped him under various symbols. Thus the tribe of Levi venerated a seraph or winged serpent, while other tribes adored a bull. The rite of circumcision, which was the symbol of the religious unity of the race, seems to have been normally practised in manhood, not in infancy. Polygamy must have prevailed as in later times, as well as the practice of blood vengeance. But we do not know whether the observance of the new moon and of the sabbath goes back to this early period.

It is inevitable that the religion of the invading Jews should have been affected by that of the Canaanites who were already settled in Palestine and whom the Jews conquered. Such influence was bound to take place, all the more as the Canaanites were also Semites and consequently already had much in common with their conquerors. A pastoral people, like the Israelites, on adopting an agricultural life, would almost necessarily adopt the religion of agriculturists. The Canaanite religion, like that of all peoples dependent on the products of the earth, would be a form of nature-worship. Hence Canaanite feasts became Israelite, and the name Baal, "lord," the Canaanite designation of god, came to be applied to Yahweh.

In order to understand their religion fully, it is necessary to sketch the history of the Jews. The sources of that history are to be found in the Old Testament, which is written in Hebrew, the national language. In the five books, called the *Pentateuch* (which in name corresponds to the *Pancatantra*, but in matter is allied to the *Mānavadharmaśāstra*) an account is given of the origin of the world and of the Jewish people from the earliest times down to their arrival in their wanderings at the southern confines of Palestine. The twelve tribes, of which Judah was one, are here traced back to the sons of Jacob (otherwise known as Israel), the son of Isaac and grandson of the Patriarch Abraham. These books also mainly contain the religious, ceremonial, social and moral laws regulating the life of the people. The book of Joshua, which forms the sixth book of the Old Testament, describes the successful occupation of Palestine by the united tribes of Israel.

In Moses, to whom the authorship of the Pentateuch is ascribed, we see the founder of Israel's religious system, Aaron being the prototype of the Israelitish priesthood.

Not long after 1000 B. C. the Jews began to be oppressed by their neighbours, also a Semitic race, the Philistines, who conquered them and seemed likely to destroy their national religion. This calamity was, however, averted by a great victory over the Philistines won by the prophet Samuel, who held supreme sway over all Israel, as the last of the Judges, until he was forced to yield to the popular clamour for a king. The choice fell on Saul, who pursued a victorious career, which, however, closed in disaster. It was his successor David who founded the monarchy of Judah at Jerusalem. The sacredness of that city dated from the installation there of the Ark as symbolizing the national religion.

Before about 850 B.C. little of the religious history of the Jews is known, but we sometimes obtain glimpses showing that the religion of this early period was of a primitive type, resembling that of some of the backward African and Asiatic races at the present day. Household gods appear to have been common. Now and then a prominent man would build a sanctuary for an idol, which would be worshipped by the family or the tribe. We have no information as to the form of these idols, but the implication is that some of them had human shape. On the other hand, it cannot be doubted that at least some of them had an animal form. High places with altars appear to have been frequent. There were also not a few larger sanctuaries with organized priesthoods, whose office tended to become hereditary. The priest was the repository of religious tradition, and the custodian of the idol where one was kept. The priests ascertained the divine will by casting lots in the presence of the idol with sacrifices and ceremonies. Beside the priests were seers and prophets, who finally became identical. The prophets proper lived in communities. There was also a class called "sacred men," whose functions in many cases at least were distinct from those of the priests. Being regarded as substitutes of the god, and being associated with the barbarous sacrifice of the first-born, they were probably of Canaanitish origin.

With about 850 B.C. the religious history of the Jews begins. When Ahab, the son of Omri was married to Jezebel, a princess of Tyre, a new danger to the country arose. Hitherto Yahweh had, at least in name, been accepted as the sole god of the nation. The attempt was now made to introduce the worship of the Tyrian Baal. Against this attempt a fierce struggle was entered upon by the prophet Elijah and then by Elisha. The result was the overthrow of the dynasty of Omri and the enforced acceptance by the nation of the doctrine: 'No god but Yahweh in Yahweh's land.' Probably at this time the ancient or earlier form of the decalogue (Exodus 34) or Ten Commandments, was drawn up in northern Israel; it was later adopted in Judah during the reign of Joash. The original draft was probably written on two stone tablets and deposited in the Ark, which contained Yahweh's image in the form of a bronze seraph. Only two of the commandments here are the same as in the later decalogue: the first being, 'Thou shalt worship no other god than Yahweh' and the fourth 'thou shalt keep the sabbath : six days shalt thou work, but on the seventh day thou shalt rest.' The remaining eight are concerned with sacrificial and ceremonial matters.

About 750 B.C. there arose a great reforming movement among the prophets in northern Israel. Just then there prevailed great religious fervour as a result of an Israelitish victory over the Aramaeans. The people thronged the temple in the hope of inducing Yahweh, by sacrifice and offerings, to give yet further proof of his love for his own people and hatred of their enemies. This religious fervour was of an entirely national character, without any ethical elements. Sacrifice at this time was regarded as an integral part of the religion of Yahweh, and the rich flattered themselves that they were propitiating Yahweh by their many offerings.

It was to a people in this condition that Amos, the first of those prophets whose teaching is collected in separate books of the Old Testament, addressed himself. Among the ancient Jews there prevailed the belief, which gave great force to the teaching of the prophets, that calamity of any sort was caused by divine displeasure. The approaching calamity which called forth the eloquence of Amos, but which was unperceived by the majority of the nation, was the impending subjugation of the states of Palestine by the growing power of Assyria. It was in this atmosphere that Amos began his movement against the practice of sacrifice. This practice he regards as a misdirection of energy. It is mercy and righteousness, he insists, that Yahweh requires, but for sacrifice he has no desire. In fact he emphasizes the ethical rather than the physical holiness of Yahweh.

Amos was soon followed by another prophet, Hosea, in the northern kingdom. Like Amos he was convinced of the futility of sacrifice. He also became the preacher not only of Jahweh's justice, but of his love. Hosea was also probably the originator of the movement which somewhat later (*c.* 700 B.C.), resulted in the introduction of the prohibition of image-worship into the law of Israel. Hosea also made an attack on the religious prostitution practised at many, if not all, the sanctuaries, in the name of Yahweh, who was thus degraded to the level of Baal. He denounced it as subversive of all morality. Amos had already denounced this highly immoral practice, but he had not attacked the worship of idols. Thus Hosea is evidently a figure of the highest importance in the moralization of the Jewish religion.

In the year 734 B.C. the Assyrians began to move against Israel under King Tiglath Pileser, and twelve years later, in 722 B.C., the kingdom of North Israel came to an end. Thousands of captives were deported, while a number of colonists were introduced from north-western Mesopotamia and other parts of the Assyrian Empire. Nevertheless the worship of Yahweh was not extinguished in northern Israel. It is probable that the destruction of the sanctuaries vindicated Hosea's teaching against idolatry and resulted in the reform which enlarged the Decalogue by the commandment forbidding the worship of images. During the latter part of the 8th century B.C. there arose a reforming movement in Judah, the southern kingdom, which had maintained its independence. Religion here was in no respect in advance of northern Israel. Thus King Ahaz was still practising the sacrifice of the first-born. At this time arose the prophet Isaiah, whose teaching was probably inspired to some extent by that of his older contemporary Hosea. He exercised great influence from 740 to 701 B.C. on the small state of Judah. Insisting on the incompatibility of Yahweh's majesty and holiness with the images by which he was represented, Isaiah gave expression to a higher conception of the divine nature. He pictured Yahweh as enthroned in his temple not as a seraph (flying serpent), but in human form, clad in a gorgeous robe, the train of which covered the whole floor of the temple, so as to leave room for no other god. He attacked the crudity of thought which could accept the bronze seraph as the representative of Yahweh. The teaching of Isaiah bore fruit, for the venerable idol, which had represented him for so long, was now destroyed. Probably at the same time the primitive decalogue, which had been accepted in the kingdom of Judah since the time of Joash, was enlarged by inserting the prohibition of idol-worship.

After the death of King Hezekiah, who had introduced some reforms, especially against idolatry, there was a violent reaction. Ancient superstitions revived, new cults were introduced by Assyrian officials and settlers, and pure monotheism seemed for the time to be lost. Nevertheless the very barbarous worship at Jerusalem was improved by foreign contact. Thus King Ahaz, as a result of his meeting the Assyrian King at Damascus in 732 B. C., had a large stone altar erected, by which the decency of the animal sacrifice was increased as compared with what had been possible when the small brazen altar was used in the Temple for the purposes of this savage practice.

In the 7th century the religion of Yahweh was in the North (in Samaria) only one of many cults. The King of Assyria allowed the return of one of the Israelite priests from exile to teach the cult of Yahweh. The sanctuary of Bethel was re-opened, and the building of altars was encouraged, because converted Aramaeans and others could not do without sacrifice, but the golden bull of Bethel no longer existed, and worship without idols was accepted by the Bethelite priesthood. The old decalogue was now combined with a collection of laws relating to slavery, property, compensation and other matters, contained in chapters 20 to 23 of the book of Exodus.

In Judah under Manasseh, who died 641 B. C., there was a reaction against reforms, but his grandson Josiah was convinced of their necessity, as he wished to stop superstitious rites at the Judaean sanctuaries. Foreign cults recently introduced were abolished, but no change was made in regard to sacrifice except that now it could be performed at Jerusalem only.

During Josiah's reign, the havoc caused in 626 B. C. by the Scythians in the north of Palestine, threatened Judah itself, and moved the prophets to preach repentance in order to avert the impending blow. The most prominent and greatest of them was Jeremiah, who for 40 years exercised wide influence in Judah. He was evidently deeply affected by the teaching of Hosea. Jeremiah remained unshaken in his conviction that sacrifice was not only unnecessary but was displeasing to Yahweh, denying even that Moses had commended it. His activities were called forth anew when a Chaldaean invasion was threatened. The King of Judah, having accepted allegiance to Nebuchadrezzar King of Babylon, before long revolted. Jerusalem was consequently invested and after a long siege was taken in 586 B. C. King Zedekiah was carried a prisoner to Babylon; the Temple and the King's Palace were burnt, and the city wall was broken down. Though the Temple was destroyed, the great stone alter of Ahaz remained. Many of the people, including priests, were deported to Babylon; but a number of the inhabitants were left, and many refugees returned. A native Jew was made governor, but he was murdered. After that Judah, like Samaria, seems to have been governed by a Babylonian official. The province of Samaria now became united for religious purposes with Judah; but the impossibility of slaughtering domestic animals except at Jerusalem was felt to be a great burden. In the 6th century B. C. important reforms connected with sacrifice and the sanctuaries were carried out. It was probably in response to Jeremiah's teaching that the sacrifice of the first-born was made illegal and their redemption compulsory. In the slaughter of domestic animals, the internal fat and the blood had hitherto been treated as most holy, the fat having to be burnt, and the blood poured out on the altar. This procedure was now simplified by requiring nothing more to be done than pour the blood out on the ground. This change removed the greatest obstacle to the requirement of the one single sanctuary being at Jerusalem.

The result of these and other reforms and concessions was the Book of Deuteronomy. The kernel is the legal code (Chapters 12 to 26). It contains a number of enactments to put a stop to superstitious and heathenish practices, as well as many ordinances dealing with matters of ordinary life. These include the different kinds of meat that may be eaten, such as that of the ox, the sheep, and the goat, and those which are forbidden, such as that of the swine.

Though this code, as requiring sacrifice, was directly at variance with Jeremiah's teaching, it did a good deal to further

Jeremiah's conception of religion. But the difficulty could not be got over that the old decalogue, which was regarded as the basis of Yahweh's covenant with Israel and which was chiefly concerned with ritual ordinances, had been repudiated by the school of Jeremiah and would never have been accepted by it as the basis of a divine 'covenant'; for it required sacrifice, but did not insist on justice, mercy, and truth. Accordingly the bold step was taken of providing a new decalogue (Deut. 5) in which were retained only the first and fourth commandments (those enjoining monotheism and the observance of the sabbath) as well as the more recently introduced prohibition of images. It was otherwise based on the ethical teaching of the great prophets, especially Jeremiah.

The law of the one sanctuary became a rallying point for the national life of Israel, as Jerusalem was now accepted as the only legitimate place of sacrifice, by the whole land which once formed the kingdom of David. The centralization of worship thus greatly developed the sense of Israelitish unity.

In the second year of Darius, king of Persia (B.C. 520), Zerubbabel, a member of the old royal family of Judah, was appointed governor of Judah. It is probable that the Deuteronomic law was adopted a short time before this.

Meanwhile among the Jewish exiles in Babylon an important development had been going on. Prominent among the priests there was Ezekiel, who felt himself called as a prophet in the 5th year of the captivity and for 22 years exercised great influence. Like other leading prophets he was convinced that the disasters of Israel were due to their sins. The chief sin he thought consisted in idolatry and idolatrous practices in the religion of Yahweh. But unlike Jeremiah he considered sacrifice to be a divine institution. He set himself to commit to writing the priestly traditions of the Temple ritual, freely introducing modifications and innovations. It was his great achievement to forge a weapon by which the religion of Israel was finally enabled to withstand the attacks of heathenism.

Of the Hebrews little remained beyond the tribe of Judah, after whom the whole race are called Jews, to return to Palestine from the Babylonian captivity. This they did in 536 B.C. From that time onwards they lived for six centuries under foreign rule, with only a short break in the period of the Maccabees, till their dispersal in the year 70 A.D. For more than two centuries (536-332), this harassed race was subject to the Persian Empire. Under that well-organized and liberal rule they enjoyed internal peace and lived under happier conditions than for long before and than ever afterwards.

Cyrus had given them leave to return; Darius allowed them to rebuild the temple, so that it was completed in the 6th year of his rule. The reign of Xerxes, under the name of Ahasuerus, was a pleasant memory. Artaxerxes I (465-424) not only allowed Ezra to return to Jerusalem in 453 B.C. with a further colony of Jews, but also sent Nehemiah there in 444 with extensive powers, such as to fortify the city. He also obtained leave to repair the wall, which was completed in 52 days. Nehemiah having been made governor of Jerusalem in 433, published in combination with Ezra a code of law which probably consisted of the whole of the Pentateuch, though it had not yet attained to its present form. It was impossible that Jews could live among the highly civilized Babylonians without acquiring a good deal of culture. Since the deportation by Nebuchadrezzar there was a real danger that religion might develop differently among the exiles in the East and those who remained behind in the West, and thus a permanent cleavage be caused in the religion of Israel. By combining the law prevailing in the East and in the West Nehemiah averted this danger. The drastic measures he took to get rid of those who would not accept the new law, which was based entirely on religious principles, transformed the population into a church rather than a nation. Priests were here all-important, the high priest being regarded as the head of the state. Nehemiah's efforts to enforce the law produced one institution inestimable for the development of spiritual religion, that is, the institution of synagogues and the rise of the class of scribes.

As the Pentateuch could not be taught at one hearing, it was necessary to provide regular instruction in it. Hence those who wished to know the will of Yahweh betook themselves not to the prophets, but to those who were duly instructed in the written law.

With the destruction of the Persian Empire in 332 B. C. the Jews came under the rule of Alexander the Great and his successors till 301 B.C. In that year they fell under the supremacy of Egypt, which had become one of the three great kingdoms arising out of Alexander's empire. Under the first three Ptolemies they enjoyed a fair amount of prosperity. Outwardly the condition of Judaism was more flourishing than it had been for centuries. There was a considerable amount of wealth among the loyal Jews. A great expansion of Judaism had also taken place, Jewish communities being settled not only in other parts of Palestine, but also among the surrounding Semitic peoples, the Ammonites, Moabites, Elamites, and Philistines. But in respect to religion, Judaism was more and more becoming a rigid ceremonial system. It was now confronted with a new and great danger. This was the rise of Hellenism which began to spread over the East.

In the year 198 B.C. Palestine became a possession of the Syrian Kingdom under Antiochus the Great. To one of his successors, Antiochus IV (Epiphanes) the Hellenistic inclinations among the Jews seemed to have prepared the ground sufficiently to enable him to carry out one of his favourite projects, the destruction of the Jewish religion and the substitution of the Olympic gods for the worship of Yahweh. In this he was encouraged by the unpopularity of the Jewish religion among the peoples of Western Asia, because of its arrogant exclusiveness towards the Gentiles, which was beginning to endanger the very existence of the nation.

Having occupied Jerusalem in 168 B.C., he issued an edic which forbade circumcision as well as the observance of the Sabbath and of other Jewish festivals, threatened the possessors of the Mosaic code with death, and ordered the worship of the Hellenic gods to be introduced both in theprovince and in Jerusalem. An altar and a statue of the Olympian Zeus led to a general insurrection of the Jews, who under the leadership of Judas Maccabaeus, were victorius. The Temple was re-dedicated in 165 B.C. and autonomy was granted under Judas's brother Simon Maccabaeus, who was accepted as High Priest in 141 B.C. The religion of Yahweh not only stood the test of this struggle, but emerged from it spiritualized and glorified. Simon's son, John Hyrkanus (135-104) had to struggle against the claims of Antiochus VII to renew the supremacy of Syria over the Jews, but finally succeeded in regaining his independence and of restoring the kingdom of David in its full extent. His death in 104 was followed by a period of external and internal conflict lasting nearly 40 years. In 65 B.C., the Roman General Pompey conquered Syria and definitely made it a Roman province. In the same year he also captured Jerusalem. As a result the Jews were under Roman supremacy for the next 135 years. It would be tedious to sketch the history of this period. Suffice it to say that the extortionate oppression of the Jews by the Roman procurator Florus led to an insurrection in 66 A.D. The ensuing war was ended in 70 A.D. by Titus the son of the Roman Emperor Vespasian, who captured and destroyed Jerusalem.

The consequence was that the remnant of the Jews disappeared from the land of their birth and was dispersed among the nations of the earth. Thus came to an end in their own country their national existence of 1000 years, two-thirds of which were spent under foreign domination. Nevertheless the Jews have, owing to the extraordinary tenacity of the race, not only preserved in exile their ancient religion practically unchanged for nearly 2000 more, but also their nationality, and in spite of many cruel persecutions in bygone centuries, have acquired great influence in the leading countries of the world. Such a fate has no parallel in the history of the world save to a very limited extent in the case of the Parsis.

Having sketched the political setting of the religion of the Jews, let us turn back to trace its development in the direction of spiritualization and morality.

The Jewish, like every other early religion, passed through the stage of polytheism. Like the other Semitic peoples, the Hebrews originally worshipped various supernatural powers, reverencing sun, moon and stars, and having a vague idea of a lord (baal) of heaven and earth But, like the other Semites, they had, besides the divine powers whom they worshipped in a general way, a special tribal god who protected them and led them in war, and to whom they felt bound to be faithful, as to an invisible tribal king. This tribal god of the Hebrews, known by the name of Yahweh, had, by the time they conquered Palestine, risen, as their victorious leader in war, to a position of pre-eminence somewhat like that of Zeus among the Olympian gods of Greece, who also finally became the only god. Monotheism, it must be remembered, is nowhere the original stage, but a later stage, the product of mature reflexion. Its development can nowhere be traced so clearly as in the religion of the Jews. Yahweh then was the chief and highest god in the earliest period, like Prajāpati in the period of the Brāhmaṇas in India. The first direct step towards monotheism was the prohibition of the right to worship any god but Yahweh, as expressed in the old decalogue; 'thou shalt worship no other god, for Yahweh is a jealous God.' The worship of Baal, the most dangerous rival of Yahweh, was destroyed about 850 B.C. in both Israel and Judah by the complete massacre of the priests of Baal; but the inherited tendency to polytheism lasted on among the people to the latest times of the monarchy. Thus even under Josiah, only 30 years before the destruction of the kingdom of Judah, we find altars of Baal, Ashtoreth, and other gods in the Temple of Jerusalem besides that of Yahweh. The worship of other gods than Yahweh has often been misunderstood as a perpetually renewed relapse from original monotheism, whereas it is obviously an inveterate clinging to an earlier stage of religion. The next and final step was the denial of the very existence of other gods, who were declared to be mere forms of stone, metal and wood. Thus by the strenuous efforts of the prophets the Jews, by about 500 B.C., accepted the belief in pure monotheism, which ever after remained one of the unshakeable pillars of Judaism. With this was associated the belief that Yahweh, having from the beginning chosen Israel among all peoples, had revealed himself to this people as the only true god.

In the character of Yahweh himself we can clearly trace a gradual development from a primitive to a comparatively high ethical conception. Here, in fact, as in all other religions, the divine character represents the personification of the ideal standard of morality prevailing in a particular period, a standard which the worshipper strives to attain. This is expressed in a general way in the Book of Genesis (1,27): 'God created man in his own image.' Translated into the language of science this means; 'men conceive God in the image of a man.' The same thing was meant by Voltaire when he said in his flippant way, 'God created man in his own image, and man lost no time in returning the compliment.' His outward form having originally been thought of as animal was soon transformed into a human one and remained so throughout the Old Testament. Even in Isaiah and the Psalms he is described as having eyes and ears, hands and feet, and so on, and as performing human actions such as seeing and hearing, sleeping and waking, breathing and smelling, speaking, crying aloud, hissing, and roaring. Many intellectual and moral qualities are attributed to him, such as thinking, resolving, remembering, anger, zeal, love, hate, compassion, joy, sorrow, and repentance. This generally anthropomorphic form and character remain throughout the Old Testament. For the people required a personal god whom they could grasp as a personification of the moral law, to whom they could speak, and to whom they could, at least in the post-exilic period, hope to be united after death.

During all the periods of the Old Testament Yahweh was regarded as the creator and preserver of heaven and earth; but that a being provided with such human qualities and functions should be capable of such activities has in modern times been criticized as a bold and even an impossible theory. It has also been pointed out that the story of the creation is contrary to nature in several respects, such as that light should be created before the luminaries which produce it, and other particulars. But the ancient Hebrews possessed too little scientific knowledge to cause any one even among the prophets to find any difficulties in such matters.

It was different in the moral sphere. Having originally been a god of war, he soon became a moral ruler who severely punished the national transgressions of worshipping other gods and practising idolatry. From his earlier character he inherited qualities such as fierce anger, vindictiveness, partial justice, hatred of other nations, occasional tendency to intrigue. These were chiefly the result of Yahweh's position as a national god. But his character was greatly moralized and spiritualized by the rise and activities of the prophets, who preached that Yahweh preferred moral purity, justice, mercy and humanity to the external ritual of bloody sacrifices.

Thus in Hosea Yahweh says: 'I desired mercy and not sacrifice, and the knowledge of God more than burnt offerings.' It was through the influence of the prophets that the Hebrew conception of God became the personification of morality and holiness, an ideal to be followed by his worshipper.

Nevertheless the nobler and deeper thinkers of the nation felt the burden of several of the difficulties which their religious system had imposed upon them, and which were only removed by their contact with the Persian religion. One of these difficulties was that Yahweh, who was good, must as creator of the world, also have created the evil of which the world is full. Thus the brooding melancholy which fell upon Saul is described as having been caused by Yahweh himself in the words: 'The spirit of the Lord departed from Saul, and an evil spirit from the Lord troubled him. Even in a passage written at the time of the Assyrian exile Isaiah makes Yahweh say: 'I am the Lord and there is none else. I form the light and create darkness, I make peace, and create evil; I the Lord do all these things.' It was only after the Jews had become acquainted with the Persian doctrine of Angra mainyu (the spirit of evil) that Satan, who had been an angel and servant of God, whose duty it was to spy out the sins of men and report them to God, was turned into an anti-divine source of all evil. This transference of evil from Yahweh to Satan is clearly seen in two parallel passages of different date. In the earlier it is written: "And again the anger of the Lord was kindled against Israel, and he moved David against them to say, 'Go, number Israel and Judah' "; and in the later: 'And Satan stood up against Israel and provoked David to number Israe'.' The idea of the origination of evil by Satan became more fully developed in the Christian teaching of the New Testament. More than the question of the origin of evil the problem of divine justice weighed on the minds of the old Hebrew thinkers. It could in fact hardly be solved on the basis of the old Jewish outlook before contact with foreign religious systems. This was because the native Jewish view of life was realistic and regarded death as practically the end of all things. There is no mention of immortality in the pre-exilic writings of the Old Testament. After death, when men had been gathered to their fathers, the dead were thought to lead a dull joyless existence in Hades (*shiol*) as shadows without blood and vitality, cut off from the upper world, and from the influence of Yahweh. The long list of promises and threats with which the two codes of Deuteronomy and Leviticus end, apply without exception to earthly life only. Similarly in all the prophets, from Amos to Malachai, who often have occasion to promise happiness to the pious and misfortune to sinners, there is no indication of the continuance of life after death.

One of the consequences of this view isthat if Yahweh, who is regarded as the ideal of justice, has not punished wrongdoers in this life, he cannot punish them afterwards, and instead has to visit his wrath on the descendants of sinners to the third and fourth generation.

It is only after contact with the Iranian religion that in late passages the idea of immortality appears in the realistic form of the resurrection of the body, as in Isaiah.

From this realistic form of a bodily resurrection of the dead must be distinguished the doctrine of the immortality of the soul which arose among the Alexandrine Jews under the influence of Greek philosophy.

Thus the Iranian doctrine of the resurrection could reconcile the old Hebrew doctrine of retribution with strict justice by transferring the requital of good and evil to a future world.

Doubts as to the justice of Yahweh did not become serious as long as he was regarded as dealing with the nation as a whole, because the sufferings of the people could be explained as due to the ineradicable inclination of the majority of the population towards the worship of other gods; but when with the decay of national life the relation of Yâhweh with the Jewish people became changed to one with the individual, the question became pressing. Thus we read in the Psalms : 'Behold these are the ungodly, who prosper in the world ; they increase in riches. Verily I have cleansed my heart in vain, and washed my hands in innocency. For all the day long have I been plagued, and chastened every morning.' And Jeremiah expostulates thus with Yahweh : 'Righteous art thou, O Lord, when I plead with thee ; yet let me talk with thee of my judgments. Wherefore doth the way of the wicked prosper? Wherefore are all they happy that deal very treacherously ?

Thinking men were coming to be convinced of the vanity of human things and to adopt one of two courses in life : either by self-abnegation to aim at a high ideal in the practice of pure justice, humanity, and renunciation, as in Buddhism ; or to enjoy life with moderation as long as possible, a view expressed in the book of Ecclesiastes ; 'there is a vanity which is done upon the earth ; that there be just men unto whom it happeneth according to the work of the wicked ; again there be wicked men to whom it happeneth according to the work of the righteous ; I said that this also is vanity. Then I commended mirth, because a man hath no better thing under the sun than to eat, and to drink, and to be merry.' This view is also expressed in the Graeco-Roman world by the poet Horace, and in ancient India by the school of the Chārvākas.

The prophets had untiringly taught that all the calamities of the Jews had been brought on them as a punishment for their defection from Yahweh, and had promised a golden age on earth as a reward for a return to his allegiance. A ruler of the house of David, a Messiah was to arise, who would make the people free, great, and happy. But these blissful days never came. The state of things only grew worse, even though the people devoted themselves from the 5th century downwards to a more stringent law of worship than ever before. An improvement in the political conditions was despaired of, and the earthly king so often expected in vain became transformed into a celestial Messiah in the clouds of the sky, and the hoped-for earthly kingdom became the kingdom of heaven. It is again the Iranian influence that has caused the spiritualization of the Messianic idea. For it appears in the Book of Daniel, which is saturated with Iranian thought and is the only one among the writings of Judaism that shows this spiritualization.

Thus we see that the conception of Yahweh, starting as that of a tribal god in a setting of polytheism, ended by the time of the Exile in pure monotheism, which remained ever after one of the two main characteristics of the Jewish religion. Similarly his character, at first that of a primitive war god, was gradually moralized to that of a partially just ruler of his people and finally to that of holiness and perfection. But this last development was reached only after certain contradictions had been removed through contact with the Zoroastrian religion.

Let us now turn to examine the relations in which the Jews stood to their god Yahweh. We have seen that from the earliest times they, like all followers of primitive religion, endeavoured to secure his favour by means of animal sacrifices and, after they had occupied Palestine, also by offerings of agricultural produce. The sacrifice generally consisted of animals divided into beasts that might be sacrificed and those that might not. The former were the animals normally used as food, especially the cow and the sheep, but also goats, turtle-doves and pigeons. The vegetables offered were those of the ordinary harvest produce. The burning of aromatic gums as incense, wine libations, and the use of oils, were also included among the offerings presented to Yahweh.

When the prophets arose, they began to inveigh against sacrifice, declaring that Yahweh was averse from such gifts, and preferred purity, justice, and mercy. Thus Hosea makes Yahweh say: 'I desired mercy, and not sacrifice; and the knowledge of God more than burnt offerings.' Again in Isaiah we read: 'To what purpose is the multitude of your sacrifices unto me? saith the Lord: I am full of burnt offerings of rams, and the fat of fed beasts; and delight not in the blood of bullocks or of lambs, or of he goats.........Bring no more vain oblations; incense is an abomination unto me; the new moons and sabbaths, the calling of assemblies, I cannot away with, your new moons and your appointed feasts my soul hateth; they are a trouble unto me; I am weary to bear them.'

Though this was the view of almost all the deepest thinkers before the period of the exile, sacrifice remained a recognized feature of the Jewish religion even afterwards. The destruction of the Temple in Jerusalem brought about a profound change. The entire divine service had come to a standstill. The priests and Levites lost their position and occupation, and to the Israelite the very centre of worship had been destroyed. The sacrifices had ceased. But the deep conviction remained among the Jews that the Temple would be rebuilt and the sacrifice re-established. In the meantime, however, have been substituted prayer, self-chastisement, and almsgiving. Thus in spite of the preaching of the prophets, sacrifice continued for a thousand years among the Jews till their national life in Palestine was destroyed. But when by the force of circumstances it became impossible, it was moralized by the substitution of more spiritual act.

I now come to the second great feature in the worship of the Jews, the complete and final abandonment of idolatry. There can be no doubt that the most faithful of the worshippers of Yahweh made use of images down to the 8th century B.C. After they settled in Palestine the Israelites proceeded in imitation of the Canaanites, the people of the country, to fabricate freely images of Yahweh and began to worship them in the public sanctuaries as well as in private.

In the sanctuaries of the Northern Kingdom Yahweh was worshipped in the form of a bull. Neither Elijah nor Elisha, nor even Amos in the 8th century thought of censuring the worship of 'golden calves.' In the kingdom of Judah, a brazen serpent, said to have been made by Moses himself, received sarifice till it was destroyed by King Hezekiah. According to Isaiah the land was full of idols. Images were kissed, greeted with incense, placed in a cell, and clothed in sumptuous garments. They were made of wood or stone or of cast metal. Those of animal form were far commoner than those of human shape.

The worship of images before very long became suspect to the upholders of the true religion of Yahweh. In the first decalogue only the worship of 'molten gods' is forbidden, the words being: 'Thou shalt make thee no molten gods,' the restriction here being perhaps due to an idea that metal images were too luxurious. The prophet Hosea was the first to lay down the incompatibility of idolatry with the true worship of Yahweh. It was probably about this time that all manufacture or worship of images of the deity was absolutely forbidden as expressed in the later decalogue: 'Thou shalt not make unto thee any graven image or any likeness of anything that is in heaven above, or that is in the earth beneath, or that is in the water under the earth; thou shalt not bow down thyself to them nor serve them.' Under Josiah all representations of Yahweh were forbidden, pagan gods being described as nothing more than wood or stone. In post-Exilic Judaism idol-worship had become definitely excluded from true religion and now remained only a popular superstition. Among the Jews who rigorously kept the law, the second commandment (which forbade idolatry) was so scrupulously followed, that all manufacture of images was avoided, even when the images were not intended for worship at all. Thus while animal representations abounded in the decoration of the pre-Exilic Temple, a perfect storm of disapproval arose when Herod introduced a golden eagle above one of the doors of the sanctuary.

In A. D. 66 the Jewish insurgents destroyed the palace of Herod Antipus at Tiberias because it was decorated with sculptures representing animals. It was out of regard for this scruple that the Romans refrained from putting human or animal effigies on coins intended for circulation in Judaea. Thus the typical spiritualized form of the Jewish religion, of which pure monotheism and the rejection of idolatry are the basis, was firmly established by the 6th century B. C. The final development of its two main features is of the highest importance in the history of civilization, because they were inherited by the two daughters of the Jewish religion, Christianity and Muhammadanism.

I now come to consider briefly, what is the relation of man to his fellow-man in the Jewish religion. The basis of Jewish morality is the standard of perfection which the conception of Yahweh's character had gradually attained in the age of the prophets. It was the attainment of this standard that is the explanation of the laws which are meant to make men, who had been formed 'in the image of God,' to reach that high standard. For Yahweh says, 'Ye shall be an holy nation' and the reason given more than once is, 'because I am holy.' The moral standard aimed at is in its main points expressed in the later decalogue, which to a considerable extent corresponds to the commandments in Buddhism. The only one relating to family life is, 'Honour thy father and thy mother that thou mayst live long.' The others relate to one's neighbour: Thou shalt not kill; thou shalt not commit adultery; thou shalt not steal; thou shalt not bear false witness against thy neighbour; thou shalt not covet anything that is thy neighbour's. The earlier view of justice between man and man is reflected in the rigid prescriptions of the Pentateuch, such as 'an eye for an eye, a tooth for a tooth.' But the books of the prophets teem with denunciations of harsh treatment of widows, orphans, and slaves, and of dishonest dealings with one's neighbours. Thus Micah says generally : 'what doth the Lord require of thee, but to do justly, and to love mercy ?' Such ethical principles and guides of life, in addition to the legal prescriptions of the *Pentateuch*, found terse expression in proverbs of wise men collected in a kind of moral compendia like the Books of Proverbs and Ecclesiastes. Much of this uncodified morality became an inheritance of the Christian religion. Thus as far as their relations to their fellow men in their own nation were concerned, the Jews had reached an advanced standard of morality.

But when we come to the wider stage of international relations, we find it was quite impossible for them to take a universal view of mankind. This was in the first place a natural result of the rooted conviction that they were the chosen people of Yahweh. This conviction produced so arrogant a contempt for the Gentiles that, as I have said, it became a positive national danger to them ; but after the dispersal this exclusive attitude became an actual necessity for the preservation of the race. Thus the very conditions of national existence precluded Judaism from developing into a religion of humanity. Such a destiny was reserved for another religion.

Selected Bibliography.

M. Friedländer, *The Jewish Religion*, London, 1891 ; I, Abrahams, *Judaism*, London, 1907, S. R. Driver, *Introduction to the Literature of the Old Testament*, Edinburgh, 1913.

LECTURE VII.

MUHAMMADANISM.

We now come to the Semitic religion called, in the West, Muhammadanism after the name of its founder, just as Christianity is after Christ. But this is not recognized as a proper expression by Muslim writers, by whom it is termed Islam or Hanifism, the designation given to it by Muhammad himself. The term Islam, which means 'submission to God,' is the religion which embraces all the different sects now existing among the followers of Muhammad. Muslim denotes those who profess this religion, including both the Shiites and Sunnites. The term Islam emphasizes the external and legal side of religion, probably never having included an ethical meaning. The term Muslim embraces various degrees of religion in the followers of Muhammad: one who carefully keeps the outward observances of the law; one who does good works as well; and one who, by adding to these sincerity of heart and the exercise of faith (*imām*), becomes a real believer.

Muhammadanism is by far the latest of the great religions of the world, having been founded in the 7th century after Christ, while King Harṣavardhana of Kanauj was reigning in India. As I have already stated in my first lecture, this religion is professed by some 175,000,000 or about 12 per cent. of the total inhabitants of the earth, its followers occupying mainly the central and south-western parts of Asia and the northern parts of Africa. Its sacred book is the Quran, written in Arabic, and composed, though not actually written or finally arranged, by its founder. It is fundamentally based on Judaism, with the additions made by its historical originator. Muhammadanism being a political as well as a religious system, it is particularly important to understand the historical circumstances under which it arose.

The career of Muhammad is known entirely from Islamic sources, which contain no contemporary biography. The earliest work that was intended to be a chronicle of his life is that by Muhammad ibn Ishag, which was written at least a century and a half after the death of the Prophet. A good deal of uncertainty therefore prevails regarding events of primary importance in Muhammad's biography. Before the foundation of Baghdad (A. D. 762) and for some time after, there prevailed among the Arabs a general suspicion of and objection to, written matter other than the Quran itself. This attitude prevented the survival of records which would have furnished a trustworthy foundation for the biography.

Though the exact year of Muhammad's birth is not recorded, we can say that it must have taken place only 2 or 3 years before 570 A. D. For a highly important event in the Prophet's career, his migration (*hijra*) from Mecca to Medina, furnished his followers with an era, 622 A. D., from which we not only know the time when Islam arose, but can calculate the dates of some other events in the Prophet's life. This era did not, however, come into use till some years after Muhammad's death. It is according to the lunar system of chronology, which was introduced into Arabia by the Prophet himself quite at the close of his career, and which displaced the previously employed solar system. On this basis we are able to state that Muhammad must have been born at Mecca either in 567 or 569 A. D., and that he died at Medina in 632 A. D., aged either 65 or 63. Muhammad's life was divided into two unequal parts by the *Hijra*, his first 53 or 55 years being spent at Mecca, the last ten at Medina. According to his biographer, Muhammad lived for 40 years as a pagan at Mecca. Here at 25 he married a woman much older than himself, who bore him one or more sons that died in infancy, and four daughters. At the age of 40 he is stated to have received from Allah revelations in which the office of prophet, or spokesman and interpreter of the deity, was conferred on him. He then for three years carried on private propaganda, gaining some adherents in his own family, among his friends, and among the lower classes at Mecca. During the next ten years he won enough supporters to be able to continue his mission publicly in the town. Towards the end of this period civil war was going on at Medina, some of the inhabitants of which invited him to settle their feuds. Accepting the invitation, he managed with difficulty to escape from Mecca, the citizens of which foresaw danger to themselves from this movement. Arrived at Medina, he organized his followers into an army and sternly suppressed all internal opposition. He then secured the alliance of various Arabian tribes and began raiding the Meccan caravans. He further inflicted several defeats on the Meccans, finally capturing their city in the 8th year after his migration. By the end of his life, two or three years later, he had imposed his doctrine on the whole of Arabia, having exterminated the Jewish communities, rendered the Christian communities tributary, and abolished paganism.

Unlike the founder of Christianity, Muhammad attained great success in spreading and establishing his new system within his own country, and that in the short period of thirteen years. This success was due to his great political ability, which showed itself in two different ways: in estimating the capabilities of others so accurately as to avoid making any mistakes in choosing his subordinates; and in utilizing to the utmost the weak points of the Arabs, with which he was thoroughly familiar. He was evidently a man of vast energy combined with patience, courage, and cadacity to seize opportunities. His moral character must be judged by the standard at that time prevailing in his own country. This appears from the acts of the Prophet recorded by his biographer, who was not an enemy and whose statements the classical traditionalists of the third Islamic century made no attempt to discredit. He could probably not have spread and established his system without the massacres which he organized and the plundering raids which he carried out after he had become the absolute ruler of Medina. But judged by the standard of modern ethics Muhammad cannot be freed from the accusation of moral unscrupulousness such as abandoning, at a certain point of his career, the doctrine of the unity of God, in order to secure a political end. And the fact that for whatever he did the Prophet was prepared to plead the express authorization of the deity must have resulted in a certain demoralization among the followers of the founder of a religion. Thus the theory that Muhammad's conduct was a model for his disciples, must have done a good deal of harm in retarding the moral progress of Islam. It is only since Muhammadans have in large numbers come under European influence and rule that Muslim communities felt the necessity of apologies on such subjects as Muhammad's toleration of polygamy and his attitude regarding slavery. From the earliest times there grew up around the figure of Muhammad much fiction which distorted his historical character and substituted a mythical one showing that the Prophet practised all the virtues admired by mankind. The process was similar in regard to Muhammad's performance of miracles. The Prophet himself disclaims on the whole the character of a miracle-worker. Though he accepted the miracles ascribed to Moses, Jesus and others, the only ones he himself claims are his victories won with the assistance of angels, and the miracle of the Quran itself as containing historical matter to which the Prophet had no natural access and which could therefore have become known to him by supernatural means only. That the Quran was composed with unattainable eloquence he also claimed as a miracle. But in time he was credited with parallels to every miracle of importance in the Old and New Testament except the raising of the dead, an exception probably due to his own resurrection never having become a dogma of Islam.

The sacred book which supplies the essential teachings of Islam is the Quran, the name most frequently used in the work itself in the form of al-Quran, meaning probably 'the lesson.' It was substantially the work of the Prophet. There is no evidence that he was seriously influenced in its composition by any of his companions, whose attitude towards him seems to have been that of worshippers. In any case, it is not likely that any of his companions had a share in its composition, because this would have been against the theory that the Suras were direct communications from the deity to the Prophet. Again, the prominent men who became associated with him after the migration to Medina and who brought about the great military success of Islam, appear to have had little or no religious conviction, many of them later becoming sovereigns, governors, or generals. There seems to be no reference in the Quran to any but oral communications of its contents. On the whole, it is difficult to suppose that it was committed to writing in the Prophet's lifetime. The claim to uniformity and consistency which it urges, is more intelligible if it is regarded like matter treated by a lecturer rather than like a permanent work published at one time as a whole. Its repetitions of the same narrative with only slight variations would otherwise be inexplicable. When the Quran had been written down, it came to be regarded as existing in heaven in the form of a book clearly distinguished from such as are written on ordinary materials. When an official copy had been circulated to the exclusion of others, a theory of verbal, and even literal inspiration, began to be evolved and ultimately prevailed. The Prophet seems to have regarded himself as speaking, not as the result of study, but by inspiration in a general sense, much as poets profess to obtain their information from the muse or similar inspirers.

The arrangement of the Quran was mainly the Prophet's, but was to a certain extent due to the second and third Caliphs. Uthman seems to have been the author of the first written edition. Usually the collection, *i.e.*, the bringing together of the parts, of the Quran (something like the formation of the Saṁhitā text of the Rigveda) is placed in the reign of the first Caliph. The editions of the Quran regularly divide the Suras or Chapters into Meccan and Medinese, but it is admitted that some Medinese matter is interpolated in Meccan Suras. Most of the Meccan Suras consist of homilies (that is, moralizing discourses) or narratives, while the Medinese are legislative and journalistic (that is, give accounts of successive contemporary events). For when Muhammad became head of a state, his Quran served as a kind of government organ, containing rescripts (*i. e.*, replies to appeals for guidance), and something like a chronicle of important events with comments on them. Before the migration from Mecca, matter of this kind was not so easily supplied, and this accounts for the fact that the Meccan part to a certain extent reproduces narratives from the Bible.

As soon as the Quran was published, it became the basis of Muslim education, being studied immediately after the acquisition of the alphabet. Public and private worship now consisted largely in repetitions of portions of it. After the Prophet's death it became the primary source of law, a school of jurists at once beginning to spring up in Medina. The difficulty of teaching the Quran to foreign converts is said to have given rise to the study of Arabic grammar. The claim of the Quran to contain a detailed accouns of everything has often led orthodox Muslim theologians to very exaggerated conclusions. Thus a certain commentator finds 10,000 problems inherent in the introductory Suras, which consist of only seven short verses.

In order to understand what Islam really was at the time of its origin without the mythological additions of tradition and commentators, it is necessary to examine the contents of the Quran as the only historically certain depository of Muhammad's own teachings Its contents are of a miscellaneous character, professing, as I have said, to include a detailed account of everything. Even though this claim is an exaggeration, we must remember that it dates from a period and nation, the civilization of which was extremely limited. Similarly, at the end of the European Middle Ages a very learned man might claim to be a master of all knowledge, whereas any such pretension would at the present day represent the very height of absurdity. The Quran consists mainly of warnings and remonstrances, of assertions or arguments in favour of certain doctrines. It also contains narratives (mostly belonging to the Meccan period) the purpose of which is to enforce morals. These narratives are for the most part accounts of events in the remote past, but there are also allusions to contemporary history and to the prophet's own experiences, being introduced for the sake of warning or apology. As the warnings chiefly refer to future punishment, the Quran abounds in realistic descriptions of both the joys of paradise and the pains of hell. It contains only a slight amount of legislation, which, as I have said, resembles rescripts rather than a systematic and consistent body of laws. It is for various reasons unsuited to be a basis of jurisprudence, being imperfect, self-contradictory, and lacking order. There are often signs of extempore treatment, even in subjects which, like the laws of inheritance, are dealt with in a comparatively methodical manner. One of the deficiencies of the Quran is that it gives no rules regarding the appointment of successors to the sovereign. This omission led to civil wars and the prevention of sound legislation till the introduction of European codes. Till then Muslims could not get rid of the notion that all law was to be got from the Quran or from the Prophet's equally inspired conduct. The Quran also contains collections of commandments in various places, and precepts on many subjects are scattered throughout the book, the most detailed being probably those concerning inheritance and adultery. A certain amount of the matter of the Quran deals with self-examination, but is expressed, as usual, in the form of personal addresses by Allah to the Prophet. In many parts, the Quran resembles a diary or commonplace book, thus furnishing materials for Muhammad's biography: but its utility in this respect is lessened by the absolute want of chronological arrangement, which it is only possible to restore conjecturally.

Translation of the Quran could not have been contemplated by the Prophet, because, as we have seen, it was not written down in his time; and Muslim sentiment has always been against such a thing being done. Though Muslim attempts in this direction have been made, nothing like an authorized version appears to have been produced in any Muslim language. There have been several translations into English; one of these is that of the late Prof. Palmer in the *Sacred Books of the East* (Vols. VI and IX).

I now come to answer the question, what were the sources of the Quran? Its material is in the main identical with the Jewish and to some extent of the Christian Scriptures, as the work itelf admits. It shows that Muhammad was familiar with a considerable part at least of the Old Testament. This knowledge was probably derived largely from the Jewish element in the population of Medina. It is in fact likely that his invitation to that town was due to this element, which was intellectually farther advanced than the Arab tribes, and which at first evidently favoured this advocate of monotheism. The Quran displays an intimate acquaintance with the books of Genesis and Exodus, out of which it reproduces numerous chapters. Its dependence on other parts of the Old Testament is much slighter, but it shows some acquaintance with the books of Judges, Samuel, and Kings, as well as with the Psalms. It also quotes an important passage from the Prophet Ezekiel. Of the other Old Testament prophets the Quran knows Elijah and Jonah, and it contains references to David and Job. The Old Testament stories most frequently told are those relating to Noah, Abraham, Lot and Moses. The story of Adam is narrated three times.

On the other hand, Muhammad's knowledge of Christianity was scanty and inaccurate. It was doubtless derived from acquaintance with the Christians of North and South Arabia, where Christianity had made progress, and perhaps from one of his predecessors in Mecca who was a relative of his wife and who had some knowledge of one of the Gospels. The only personages belonging to the New Testament mentioned in the Quran are Zecharias, John the Baptist, the Virgin Mary, Jesus and the angel Gabriel. It narrates the account of the birth of Christ twice.

Matter or phrases that occur in the Old Testament, the New Testament, the Talmud, or the New Testament Apocrypha, are found throughout the Quran. This reproduction is sometimes close enough to justify the term 'quotation.' But the quotations are inaccurate, and the manner in which they are introduced implies that the writer had only a vague notion of the book cited. It is in fact improbable that any part of the Biblical matter of the Quran was obtained by Muhammad at first hand from books. For there is no evidence either that any part of the Bible had been translated into Arabic before the rise of Islam, or that the Prophet had studied any language but his own. It has even been doubted whether Muhammad could read and write; but the evidence indicates that he could do both, though not well. The form in which the proper names and technical terms appear in the Quran, indicates that they are borrowed from at least four different languages: Hebrew, Syriac, Greek and Ethiopic. For instance, the name

Shaitan, the English form of which is Satan, comes from Ethiopic; and *Iblis*, the name of the chief of the devils, can be phonetically traced to Greek through the Syriac transliteration. Again, from the manner in which the Bible narratives are told, it is difficult to imagine that the writer was acquainted with the continuous history of the Bible; for he knows only stories out of it. From all this it may be inferred that Muhammad heard the Biblical stories from narrators of different nationalities who translated them orally into Arabic; and that what was reproduced during the Meccan period Muhammad had heard from travelling companions or from Jews and Christians whom he had met during his tours; while the positive part of his teaching was largely derived from the Judaism which he found prevailing at Medina when he migrated thither. During Muhammad's lifetime the publication of the Quran took an evolutionary form, coming out as required by circumstances in parts which were gathered together in the form of a complete book some time after the Prophet's death.

It is somewhat difficult to say how much Muhammad derived from the paganism of the Arabian tribes which was displaced by his system, for we do not know enough about their religious beliefs in detail. But our knowledge of Semitic religion in general makes it likely that these communities had their tribal and local cults before their abolition by Muhammad through the introduction of monotheism as a preliminary step towards the political union of Arabia. He adopted the name of Allah as that of the one and only deity from one of the Arabian tribes, though of course dropping the accompanying female deity Al-lat. He probably retained general Arabian customs that were not in conflict with his main doctrines. Thus in adopting Mecca as a centre of pilgrimage he merely stereotyped the practice of Arabic tribes in visiting the temple at Mecca containing the Black Stone. And in connexion with this he even retained an idolatrous custom, which, as not very obviously having this character, was an aid towards the unification of Arabia, and which survives even to the present day in Islam.

Muhammadanism has been, like Buddhism and Christianity, a missionary religion from the beginning. When the Prophet had begun the policy of winning the Arab tribes, missionaries were sent out to teach those parts of the Quran which were employed in the Muhammadan liturgy. These missionaries were not altogether of a religious type, but were to some extent of a military character. This aspect of the emissaries of Islam showed itself particularly when the time had come to extend the mission outside Arabia. Envoys were then sent with copies of a letter from the Prophet addressed to all monarchs known to him. As these contained a command to adopt Islam on pain of being attacked, there was no occasion for the messengers to use persuasion. Here we already see the application of the policy which is apparent throughout the course of Islam, the principle of propagating the religion by force rather than suasion, in contrast with the two other great missionary religions, Buddhism and Christianity. The political colouring of early Islam is also borne out by the later careers of the leading adherents of the Prophet. They accumulated fortunes and otherwise obtained conspicuous worldly success. Several of them distinguished themselves as commanders of armies. There was much rivalry for first place among them, and twenty-five years after the Prophet's death some of his companions led armies against each other. All these rival military commanders were in later legends transformed into saints and preachers, and sometimes even ascetics.

Before leaving the subject of the Quran I ought to say a few words about its literary form and its place in Arabic literature. The revelations embodied in it were, according to tradition, made by the Deity to the Prophet and uttered by the latter in a condition of trance. The form of the utterances approaches verse, in which rhyme is loosely used. The Prophet himself claimed to introduce literature into his native language with the Quran. This is probably correct in the sense that it was the first large and connected work in Arabic. It is on the whole unlikely that the Arabs to whom the Quran addressed itself had, beyond some primitive poetry, any native literature. For the Quran constantly states that it had not. This is in fact probably one of the causes of Muhammad's rapid success. For he had thus nothing to overthrow except immemorial custom. In the Meccan period the Prophet was regarded as a poet by his countrymen. This attribution is however, vehemently repudiated in the Quran, partly perhaps because poets were thought to be inspired by *jinns*, or devils.

In the first century after the Hijra, the Prophet's sayings and doings began to be accumulated as a source of law when the system of jurisprudence was established by the labours of jurists in Medina. But the great collections of the Prophet's precedents and rulings date from about 900 A.D. Thus what is genuine and what is apocryphal cannot be separated. Muhammad's merits as a legislator must be judged exclusively by the Quran; for there is little reason for thinking that the rest of the sacred code ascribed to him is his work.

The Prophet is supposed to have expressed opinions on all sorts of subjects, as for instance on medicine. Those bearing on virtues and vices were collected on a large scale, about 1100 A.D. by Ghazali in his *Revival of the Religious Sciences*, the standard textbook of orthodox Islam theology. The compiler of this work has, however, been severely criticized for the incorporation, in his collection, of many spurious dicta which can be traced to fabricators. Here again the Quran is in the moral sphere the only safe ground as the source of Muhammad's own work.

After this historical survey of the origins of Islam, we may now turn to an account of its main religious and ethical teachings. Tradition shows that the chief doctrines of Islam were slowly developed. It is probable that the only part of Muhammad's religious scheme that never varied was the restoration of the religion of Abraham, to whom the descent of the Arabs was traced. Thus when the Prophet decided to make the pilgrimage to Mecca part of his system, he ascribed the building of the Kaba temple to Abraham and Ishmael. The earliest of the main doctrines of Muhammad's teaching were the unity of God, the folly of idolatry, and the future life.

Monotheism seemed to the Prophet the most valuable means of bringing about the political unity of the Arabian tribes by destroying all local cults. But the one and only God himself had nevertheless to be treated as a tribal god on an enlarged scale, favouring the Arabic community, but hostile to all others. This was doubtless the conception of Allah that attracted many of the able men who, after the Hijra, joined Muhammad, and being moved by admiration for the Prophet's military and diplomatic skill, were anxious to serve under so gifted a chief. For they regarded Allah as leading the Muslims in war, as able to defeat all other communities, and always ready to listen to the Prophet's call for divine aid. The monotheistic doctrine had not yet become an unshakeable one during the Meccan period. For according to Tabari, the Prophet at one time under stress issued a revelation admitting the Meccan goddesses to his pantheon, and though this text was expunged from the Quran, the apology for it as the devil's interpolation remains. But later, the doctrine of Allah as the one and only God became as firmly established as that of Yahweh from the time of the exile in Judaism.

Muhammad's campaign against idolatry was surprisingly successful. When we consider the long and strenuous struggle which was carried on for centuries in Israel with a view to the suppression of idols, the ease with which

Muhammad induced the Arabs to abandon their gods and goddesses is remarkable, for there appears never to have been a revival of paganism in Arabia. It is a great tribute to Islam that it is the only religion, except Zoroastrianism, which succeeded in maintaining throughout the spiritual purity of its monotheism, and never relapsed to the lower level of image-worship. Such degeneration is to be found not only in Buddhism, but even in some forms of Christianity: in the eikon-worship of the Greek Church and in the Mariolatry of the Latin races. There is, however, just one survival of paganism connected with idolatry in Islam: the kissing of the Black Stone at Mecca. Though not mentioned in the Quran, it forms an Islamic pilgrimage rite. The early Arabs are known to have kissed the image of a god as a recognized form of adoration; and so at Mecca they kissed the Black Stone, which is believed by Muslims to be one of the stones of paradise. This rite was retained by Muhammad in his system, probably as a concession to a harmless ancient national custom which would emphasize the sanctity of Mecca and serve as a unifying element in Islam.

The doctrine of the future life was preached by Muhammad in the early days of his mission as a warning of the approaching end of the world and of the day of judgment. This doctrine is evidently borrowed from post-exilic Judaism, which as we have seen derived it from Persia. The resurrection is described in this way. At death the body again becomes earth, while the soul sinks into a state of sleep or unconsciousness. On a day decreed, an angel will sound a trumpet, the earth will be broken up, and the soul will rejoin the body. Allah will appear on his throne surrounded by angels. The great book will be opened and a list of his deeds, good and evil, will be given to every man. A balance will be used to weigh the deeds. The *jinns* will testify against the idolaters. The righteous will then obtain eternal peace and joy in the garden, while the wicked will be cast into the fiery ditch, where pain of body and of soul will be united. This view of the future life, in which, after a long period of unconsciousness, there took place a remote resurrection followed by reward in heaven and punishment in hell, was afterwards modified by Muhammad inasmuch as he made the martyrs in his cause enter paradise at once, and his enemies enter hell immediately after death. In the earliest form of Islam, besides the negative prohibition of idolatry certain positive daily ceremonies were prescribed. Thesa were afterwards developed and finally became stereotyped as the five regular forms of worship.

The other canons or main institutions of Islam which belong to the later or Medina period, are the pilgrimage to Mecca, the fasting month of Ramadan, and the charity tax. These are obviously connected with outward religious observances, while those of the earliest period represent fundamental spiritual doctrines.

The establishment of the pilgrimage to Mecca indicated the Prophet's intention to conciliate as far as possible the pagans of his native place, and to abandon Judaism, which on his arrival at Medina he was inclined to adopt. His motive was similar in making the Meccan temple, instead of Jerusalem, the direction in which the worshipper turned during prayer. Such measures, as I have already indicated, helped Muhammad's policy of unifying the Arabian tribes.

The fasting month, the exact origin of which is uncertain was evidently introduced to serve as a military exercise, accustoming the fighting men to endure privation and training them to turn night into day. It is not connected with the principle of asceticism, which is characteristic neither of Islam nor of its founder. Fasting is enjoined in the Quran as a penance for certain ritual and legal offences. It was Christianity, not ecclesiastical, but of an irregular and unorthodox type, that sowed the first seeds of asceticism in

Arabia, before the advent of Muhammad. According to the Quran, monasticism was an innovation in Christianity itself, and Muhammad declared that it was no part of Islam. At a later time, however, asceticism became firmly established in Islam and had to be reconciled with the Prophet's teaching. It was the almost unendurable conditions produced by the long and bloody civil wars and the fierce fanaticism of the political sects after the Prophet's death, that turned men's minds in disgust from earthly affairs, encouraged the growth of asceticism, and led to the establishment of Sufi monasteries about 200 years after the *Hijra*.

The institution of the charity tax of 2½ per cent. on income was meant as a system of organized poor relief to take the place of unregulated almsgiving.

At least as important as any of the canons, though not called one, was the prohibition of intoxicants, which is said to have been introduced three years after the migration to Medina. The institution of abstinence from intoxicating liquor is a very valuable feature of Islam, and has had a beneficent influence in the diffusion of Muhammadan civilization. This important prohibition was also a feature of Buddhism as we have seen, more than 1,000 years before the rise of Islam. It is, in my opinion, to be regretted that a similar prohibition was not adopted in the early stage of Christianity, as so much social evil is to be traced to indulgence in intoxicants in European countries. Such a prohibition by the founder of a religion seems to have resulted historically in general abstinence in this respect, while the effort to enforce it by democratic legislation at the present day does not seem to promise simliar success. The American nation with a population of 100 millions in the United States, has adopted it in this manner ; but the law is evaded to such an extent that it seems somewhat ineffective for the present at least. We must wait for the slow advance of civilization to complete this reform.

Let us now turn to Muhammad's conception of Allah in his relations with man. This, as in other religions, reflects the moral standard of the Prophet's time and nation. His deity is on the whole mainly anthropomorphic. The Allah of the Quran has been compared with a magnified Oriental despot. On the whole he resembles the earlier conception of Yahweh in Judaism. He is more spiritual than the two leading gods of the Rigveda ; but he is like Indra in the quality of capriciousness, while Varuṇa's sway resembles more the uniformity of the laws of nature. In making such comparisons it must be remembered that the Vedic gods are chronologically about 2,000 years older than Allah. The latter has a royal court which is formed by angels, some of whom remind one of the spies of Varuṇa. One of these angels is Gabriel, who conveys messages to the Prophet, while others are sent, mounted on horses, to fight his battles. Other intelligent beings under Allah are the *jinns* or Shaitans, whose prince is Iblis. This chief of the devils is the power that makes for evil, causes men to forget, and even introduces interpolations into the Quran. He has Allah's permission to mislead mankind for a season. The figure of Shaitan (or Satan) is evidently borrowed from post-exilic Judaism, which as we have seen, derived it from Persia.

Allah's general attitude is that of the strict justice of the Mosaic Law, which the Quran quotes in the form of the rule : 'soul for soul, eye for eye, nose for nose, ear for ear, tooth for tooth.' But we also find the old vindictive justice of the Mosaic Law modified by the influence of a saying of the Prophet Ezekiel : 'The soul that sinneth, it shall die. The son shall not bear the iniquity of the father, neither shall the father bear the iniquity of the son : the righteousness of the righteous shall be upon him, and the wickedness of the wicked shall be upon him.' This appears in the Quran expressed in the form : 'no burdened soul shall bear the burdens of another, and there is nothing accounted to a man save what he has wrought.' But Allah, though ordinarily requiring strict justice, was regarded as having full power to overlook evil deeds, if he so willed, like any despotic ruler, but as allowing no merit to the unbeliever, however moral his action. The teaching of the Quran on the whole seems to favour the theory of predestination, that is, the doctrine that Allah appoints from eternity some of mankind to salvation, others to damnation. This is a kind of fatalism, another form of which appears in the Hindu doctrine of *Karma*. But in the case of *Karma* it acts with absolute uniformity, like a law of nature, subject to no interference by divine caprice. Allah is regarded as a Creator, practically of the same type as Yahweh in Judaism. The story of Creation is, indeed, narrated in the Quran mainly as in the first chapter of Genesis in the Old Testament. After death Allah assigns an existence of bodily joys and pains, the Quran scarcely touching metaphysical questions concerning the soul.

The relation of Muhammad himself to Allah was that of his Prophet, into whose heart the Quran was brought down from heaven by the 'Faithful Spirit' called Gabriel. Revelation in the Muhammadan sense seems to mean the mental perusal by the Prophet of the divine book which is in heaven and the contents of which he communicates to his countrymen. Muhammad's first conception of a prophet was much the same as that which prevailed among the Hebrews before the literary prophet had arisen. Like the Hebrew prophet he was a 'warner,' an epithet which he applied to himself. His method of foretelling misfortunes was generally that of predicting what would happen if the line of conduct which he recommended were not followed. Muhammad never claimed for himself a divine nature, nor to be more than a human being. When he became acquainted with the division in Christendom on the subject of the nature of Christ, he vehemently rejected the doctrine of his divinity, though he accepted his virgin-birth and his ascension to heaven while alive. But he rejected the doctrine of Christ's Resurrection, for he denied that Christ had been crucified. He did not indeed understand the position of Jesus in Christianity, for he supposed that the Christian worshipped three deities: Allah, the Virgin Mary, and Jesus, whom he identified with the spirit of God, but also called 'the Word,' a term which he evidently obtained from the fourth Gospel of the New Testament.

Man's relations with Allah have five aspects in Islam: the recital of the creed; the observance of the five daily prayers; the fast of the month Ramadan; the giving of the legal alms; and the pilgrimage to Mecca. The creed of Islam is, as you probably all know, the expression of the belief that: 'there is no god but Allah; Muhammad is the Apostle of Allah.'

There is one religious institution of Islam which though directly borrowed from Judaism, was considerably modified by Muhammad: the observance of the Sabbath day. He not only shifted the Sabbath from Saturday to Friday but reduced the time when business might not be carried on to the period occupied by the midday religious service.

Let us now turn to the ethical side of Islam, that which concerns the relations of man to his neighbour. The position of the family does not appear to have differed materially from that which prevailed before the appearance of the Prophet. Polygamy and concubinage were retained and recognized as normal. It is, however, uncertain whether the text which is supposed to limit the number of wives to four was intended to have that meaning. During his Meccan period Muhammad himself had only one wife, Khadija, whose acceptance of her husband's claim to a supernatural mission was an important element in determining its success. She is said to have died shortly before the Prophet's migration to Medina. After her death, Muhammad, in his second period, embarked on a course of polygamy and concubinage, which, however, does not appear to have scandalized his Arabian contemporaries, doubtless because there was nothing abnormal about the practice at the time. But there was one exception that caused offence, his marriage with the wife of his adopted son. This episode is said to have been the cause why the statute of adoption was never recognized in the system of Islam. This marriage is defended in a Quranic revelation. In several of his marriages political considerations were evidently dominant, as Muhammad, like other leaders, wished to unite his chief helpers to himself by as many bonds as possible, and to get a hold on dangerous opponents. His favourite wife, Ayeshah, the daughter of his most faithful follower, Abu Bekr, played a historical part of great importance, and in the first civil war, herself took the field. Through his daughter Fatima (by his first wife) his descendants have been distinguished for rather more than 500 years by the wearing of green turbans. It is uncertain how far the seclusion of women, which has for a great many centuries been a feature of Islam, was enjoined or countenanced by Muhammad himself. The 17th chapter of the Quran contains a short account of its chief ethical requirements. As regards the relation of parents and children it is there said : 'The Lord has decreed kindness to one's parents whether one or both of them reach old age with thee, and say not to them "Fie," and do not grumble at them, but speak to them a generous speech. And lower to them the wing of humility out of compassion and say, "O Lord, have compassion on them as they brought me up when I was little." Honour to parents is in several Suras given a high place in the list of commandments. Again, in the treatment of children by parents, Muhammad introduced a great moral reform by abolishing infanticide, which according to the Quran was commonly practised in Arabia in the case of female infants. The words referring to this in the 17th Sura are: 'slay not your children for fear of poverty ; we will provide for them ; beware ! for to slay them is ever a great sin.'

As regards kinsmen the Quran enjoins equitable treatment, as in the words, 'give thy kinsman his due.' But he still tolerates the blood-feud, though without vindictiveness, saying: 'for him who is slain unjustly, we have given his next of kin authority; yet let him not exceed in slaying.' Thus though he did not contemplate complete abolition of blood-feud, he endeavoured to mitigate its results, and favoured mild reprisals.

In dealing with the conduct of man to man, the Quran scarcely formulates any general principle of morals, but on the whole insists on moderation, without aiming at any considerable departure from current notions in such matters. Thus in the general constitution of society he acquiesces in the institution of slavery, which has remained ever since his time a recognized element of Muslim society. He even deprecates extravagance in almsgiving as in other matters. He found no fault with the institution of private property and the acquisition of wealth. Muhammad in fact appears, as I have already indicated, to have had no leaning towards ascetic morality which was afterwards taught by Sufi preachers; for it finds little support in any interpretation of the Quran and clearly receives no countenance from the Prophet's own career.

Several of the commandments regulating social life which are enjoined in the Quran, are virtually identical with those of the Mosaic law. Such is the prohibition of murder: 'Slay not the soul that God has forbidden you, except for just cause.' Adultery is forbidden with the words: 'Draw not near to fornication; verily, it is ever an abomination, and evil is the way thereof.' Abstention from covetousness and dishonesty are enjoined: 'Draw not near to the wealth of the orphan, save to improve it, until he reaches the age of puberty, and fulfil your compacts; give full measure when ye measure out, and weigh with a right balance.' Theft is denounced. The *tabu* of intoxicants was a valuable addition to Muhammad's moral code, for it has doubtless exercised a beneficent influence in the history of Islam. On the other hand, his institution of compensation for oaths, that is to say, the principle that an oath might be violated at the pleasure of the person who had sworn it, if he performed some sort of penance, has caused serious harm to Islam.

One of the virtues inculcated in the Quran is humility, as expressed in the injunction: 'walk not on the earth proudly; verily thou canst not cleave the earth, and thou shalt not reach the mountains in height.' Another virtue that Muhammad rated very high was personal courage, and though he often inspired it by the promise of paradise, most of his personal followers required no such stimulus. But such instigation was of great importance in the later history of Islam, the conquering force of which was thereby greatly increased.

One of the institutions that affected the general social life of Islam was the *tabu* of certain kinds of food. Though Muhammad went out of his way to record in the Quran what he supposed to be the Jewish rules on the subject of forbidden foods, he adopted instead of the elaborate system so prominent in the Mosaic code, the minimum retained by the council of Jerusalem, with the prohibition of swine's flesh added.

In the inter-tribal and international relations of mankind Islam showed a distinct advance as compared with the attitude of other branches of the Semites. Muhammad's monotheistic reform, combined with the establishment of Mecca as the religious centre of the system, turned the Arabian tribes into an Arabian nation, just as the monotheism of the Jewish tribes, with Jerusalem as a religious centre, had welded those tribes into a Jewish nation more than 1,000 years before. Yet he failed to make the Muslim life as inviolable within the Muslim world as the tribesman's life had been in the single tribe. For soon after his death civil war broke out, and massacres of Muslims by Muslims took place. But by subordinating nationality to religion Islam went further than Judaism, for it produced a feeling of brotherhood between nations as long as they were united within the limits of the Muslim religion. But it failed to reach the conception of the brotherhood of humanity which had been attained by Christianity six centuries earlier; for such universality would only have been possible in Islam if the whole world had embraced that religion. Friendship with members of other communities is forbidden. Muslims are told to fight with other communities relentlessly until they accept Islam or pay tribute, which they are to bring in humiliation. It is significant that the most intolerant utterances are the latest ones. The ultimate system adopted was to permit the existence of communities which professed to follow a revealed book, but to disarm them and make them tributary. Such an attitude shows no sign of an approach to an outlook embracing all mankind.

In summing up, the general statement may be made that as a religion, Islam represents a modified form of Judaism, but that as a system of morality it stands partly on the same level as Judaism (as in institutions such as polygamy and slavery) and partly midway between Judaism and Christianity. It goes beyond the Jewish outlook, which is limited to its own nationality; for it admits other nations to brotherhood, but only within the limits of its own religion. It falls short of the outlook of Christianity which includes all mankind. Its propagation to other nations is based not on persuasion, but on political aggression.

It cannot be denied that Islam has raised to a higher level of civilization not only the Arabs but many other backward races. This it has effected to a large extent by the astonishing pertinacity with which it has been able to uphold its two main doctrines that make for spirituality: monotheism and the rejection of idolatry. But it has suffered from the defect of arrested development caused by the sacred book that contains its doctrines and laws having been written down at the time of its origin. These, though representing an advance at the period of the rise of Islam, are scarcely capable of adapting themselves to the progressive and complex forms of modern civilization. Thus Muhammadanism does not possess the characteristics which would qualify it to become a universal religion.

Selected Bibliography.

F. A. Klein, *The Religion of Islâm*, London, 1906; D. B. Macdonald, *Aspects of Islâm*, New York, 1911.

LECTURE VIII

CHRISTIANITY.

We now come to the last of the great religions with which we are concerned, Christianity, the religion of the West, which undoubtedly represents one of the greatest phases of human evolution. It has had an immenese influence there on politics, literature, and philosophy; and it has moulded the minds and characters of many of the most distinguished men who have adorned the human race. From the earliest period of its history, Christianity was, like Buddhism and Islam, a missionary religion, and has continued to be so down to the present day. In modern times it has come into contact with ancient civilizations of the East, as well as with barbarism in all parts of the earth, by conquest, colonization, and commerce. Through European civilization, in the making of which it has been a powerful factor, it has begun to affect the life of all mankind, of which its adherents already form a large proportion. Thus at the present day, according to the estimate of Dr. Feller, an eminent German statistician, there are 534, 940,100, Christians, *i.e.*, about 35 per cent., out of 1,544,500,000, the total population of the world. Within the nations that profess Christianity the moral and social progress, which was especially conspicuous in the last century, has been very largely inspired and directed by the Christian ideal. In higher moral standards, in progressive social reform, and till the outbreak of the Great War, in improved international relations, this influence can be traced, though of course other factors were also at work. On the other hand, the Christian Church as an institution, has not the same hold on the bulk of the population as it had a hundred years ago. This is probably due to a growing distaste for what seem barren theological controversies on dogmas and for petty sectarian differences, and an increasing preference for the broader aspects which are concerned with the realities of human life.

At this point you may ask for a general definition of Christianity. Well, we may define it briefly as a monotheistic religion, which was founded by Christ on the basis of Judaism, the faith of the Jews, in which Christ appears as a mediator between God and man, in which mankind is redeemed by the sacrificial death of Christ, and which, in its religious and moral scope, embraces the whole of mankind. It has been a great advantage to the diffusion of Christianity that it is based on the life and sayings of Christ, and was not tied down by a body of rules and regulations, such as the laws of Moses or the Quran of Muhammad. It was therefore able to adapt itself to the evolution of mankind, to influence civilization, and not to be trammelled by ideas and customs which, being derived from a less advanced state of society, no longer harmonize with the times and therefore ought to be cast off.

I now propose first to sketch the history of Christianity, then indicate its main religious doctrines, next its moral or practical side, and lastly its present and its future tasks in the interests of humanity.

1. The history of Christianity may in general be divided into three eras. In the first or ancient period, the Christian Church spread from Jerusalem to Rome, from Rome to the whole Roman Empire, and on the fall of that Empire, to the Germanic nations. This period covered the first eight centuries. In the second or mediaeval era, which lasted 700 years, the power of the Pope grew until it became supreme in Western Europe; but it then began to decline in the 13th century, when various movements towards reform appeared. The third era, beginning in 1517 with Luther's theses against indulgence, is not yet closed.

The ancient era may conveniently be described in 4 sub-divisions.

a. The first of these is the Apostolic Age, embracing a century (1-100 A. D.). Christ founded the new religion on the basis of Judaism, accepting the ethical monotheism of the Hebrew Prophets. The New Testament, written in Greek, is the only source for the beginnings of Christianity that need be considered. The epoch in which this religion arose was a most timely one. For it soon came into contact with the Greek world, the religious and moral thought of which had become peculiarly well adapted for the reception of the similar ideas and doctrines of Christianity. Its greatest and most energetic apostle, St. Paul, was a man brought up in the atmosphere of Greek culture. The civilization of Greece had long before this permeated the Roman Empire, so that this widest and most civilized united area of the ancient world lay open for its reception. But the most indispensable condition of the diffusion of Christianity was to be found in the fact that the greatest civilization the human race had seen lay in its death throes, involving the loss and ruin of the old philosophy and knowledge. Having no longer any firm beliefs, the people of the Roman Empire began to think that a religion, for which its votaries were ready to sacrifice ther lives must have a deep significance. But for these favourable circumstances Christanity could hardly have become a world-religion, and Western Europe might still be steeped in barbarism. In this first century the Christian Church became completely severed from the Jewish people.

b. During the second and third centuries, Christianity progressed throughout the Roman Empire in spite of repeated persecutions, until in 313 A. D. the Emperor considered itpolitic to strengthen his position by adopting this religion as his own.

c. In the third sub-period embracing nearly three centuries (313-590) the Christian Church became supreme in the Roman world.

d. In the fourth sub-period (590-800) the outstanding features were the founding of the Church among the Germanic nations, on the one hand, and the conquest of many of the Christian lands of the East by Islam, on the other.

II. The second main (mediaeval) era begins with the crowning of Charlemagne, the King of the Franks, by the Pope in 800. The dominating interest of the Middle Ages is the contest for supremacy between Emperor and Pope.

In the Mediaeval period occurred the Great Schism, by which the 'Holy Orthodox Church' of the East, the Greek Church in Constantinople, became separated from the Catholic Church of the West in Rome, as the political separation into an Eastern and Western Empire had taken place centuries before.

Monasticism, being very prevalent, exercised a most powerful influence in the Middle Ages. Arising from worthy motives, and for a time serving useful ends, it grew more and more corrupt, and was denounced by the Reformers. It was evidently a highly anti-social institution. For much was lost to mediaeval society by the withdrawal from family life and citizenship of the best men and women.

A strange and sad phenomenon, though ennobled by much heroism, appeared in this age: the seven Crusades between 1096 and 1270, in which Christendom endeavoured to recover from Islam the sacred places of its religion. Though the direct result was disastrous, the Crusades had at least the effect of widening the horizon of Christianity and deepening its sense of unity.

In this period arose many sects to oppose the claims of the clergy. In consequence, the tribunal of the Inquisition was founded in 1232 to deal with heresy. It was entrusted to the order of the Dominicans, who by a pun were called the *Domini canes*, the dogs of the Lord.

These three phenomena of the Middle Ages, its monasticism, its Crusades, its Inquisition, all proceeding from more or less worthy motives, resulted in great waste of goodness, in much bloodshed, unhappiness and suffering. They were really all due to various forms of ignorance inevitable in the evolution of religion and morality, but likely to disappear as the world progresses.

III. The third or modern period begins in 1517, when the reform movement, reinforced by the Renaissance or revival of learning, which followed the capture of Constantinople in 1453, and the consequent diffusion of Greek learning in Western Europe, was brought to a head by Luther. From that time dates the existence of Protestantism in the Germanic countries: England, Scotland, north Germany, Holland, Scandinavia, Switzerland, and North America.

Christianity, having its source in the life and activity of its founder Jesus Christ, is a historical religion like Confucianism, Zoroastrianism, Buddhism and Islam. Like Buddhism and Islam, it is also a missionary religion. But unlike all the others, it is the only one that can be said to be a universal religion, in the fullest sense one that appeals to the whole human race, though it is derived from one that was emphatically national, Judaism. Though both Buddhism and Islam claim to be universal in character, neither, when examined more closely, shows itself to be completely adaptable to the needs of a universal religion. Buddhism as a monastic and therefore anti-social system, with its pessimistic aversion from human activity, is evidently unfitted for the rôle of inspiring and directing any progressive society. Islam too, is, both in its creed and code, so bound up with the peculiarities of early Arab thought and life, that without undergoing a thorough transformation, it could not be expected to win acceptance in any highly cultured and civilized society, though it has shown itself well adapted to the religious needs of less advanced populations. The history of Christianity seems to show that, generally speaking, it meets the cravings of the individual human soul better than any other system, while both in its religious and its moral aspect it has proved itself more adaptable to every stage of civilization than either of the other missionary religions at the present day. Even to those who may have rejected many, or possibly all, its religious dogmas, it leaves as a result of its influence, a higher moral standard than either of the others is capable of. In expressing this view I must not be taken to depreciate other religions. Far from it. I consider Buddhism in its original form a noble religion, in various respects equal to any other.

Christianity shares with Judaism and Islam the characteristic of being a monotheistic religion, but the character of the monotheism is different in all three. Its conception in Judaism is still closely bound up with the peculiarities of national custom, Yahweh being exclusively the God of the Jews, not of mankind in general. The monotheism of Islam shows a defective moral idea of the divine character, and Allah, though not regarded as the god of one nation only, is still limited as the god of one particular religion. Christ accepted the Old Testament or Jewish idea of God, but carried it to a further stage of development. He revealed God as a Father both of Himself and of mankind; and the impression which his personality made on the religious community he founded, led to the Christian conception of one God in the aspects of Father, Son, and Spirit. This is the doctrine of the Trinity, or as it is better called, Tri-unity. It may be said that the unequalled potency of Christianity as a religion of the heart has always consisted in this very conception of the Man-God Jesus Christ. But the unity of God is a cardinal doctrine of Christianity, which is therefore essentially monotheistic.

Another characteristic of Christianity is that it is redemptive, in other words, that it is Christ who redeems or delivers men from evil. Men early became conscious of the reality of physical evil in various forms, from which they desired to be protected and delivered. As their moral development advanced they also became conscious of moral evil or sin in themselves, and felt the need of being saved from it. No religion can satisfy the whole man, unless it offers him redemption or deliverance from evil, physical or moral, whichever he may feel most keenly. The 'enlightenment' of Buddha consisted in discovering the secret of salvation. He laid stress on physical evil, regarding it as inseparable from existence. The deliverance he offered is annihilation. This deliverance is effected by man himself without any assistance from divine agencies. Christianity, on the other hand, emphasizes moral evil as the root of man's unhappiness, and offers deliverance from sin, by the grace of God, through the sacrificial death of Christ, promising an immortality of bliss with God.

Christ's mediation between man and God is the central point of Christianity. In this mediation the sacrifice of Christ is an essential factor. Thus Christ occupies an altogether unique position. He is not only teacher and example as Buddha was, but by his own death offered the sacrifice by which men are delivered from moral evil or sin. It is as if one of the Avatars of Viṣṇu saved mankind not from a great physical calamity by some mighty deed, as in the Fish incaranation from the flood, but from moral death and damnation by the sacrifice of his own life. It is as if *mokṣa,* or deliverance from the continuation of evil and sin, were obtained not by some form of enlightenment achieved by man's own efforts, but by the death of a saviour who thus restored him to communion with God.

It is to be borne in mind that several doctrines of Christianity grew up and were formulated in the early centuries of our era, and were long accepted without question, but they have begun to be rejected in recent times as contrary to the true spirit of Christianity.

As there is no agreement concerning many of the dogmas

of Christianity, these can hardly be considered essential, and they may be left to the controversial handling of theologians. The rest represent the spirit rather than the forms of the religion, and as they bear on the mental and social happiness of the human race, they come within the sphere of practical Christianity.

Christian morality or practical Christianity is based on the life and sayings of Christ, as recorded in the New Testament, which, however, contains no formal system of ethics. This, as I have already indicated, is very fortunate, because much that was important only for the age when Christianity arose, would have been a retarding influence in later times, while as it is, the general spirit of Christianity has been able not only to adapt itself to changing circumstances, but to act as a potent factor in the progress of civilization.

The leading principle of the Christian religion, charity, or love of one's follow men, runs through its morality also. It is expressed in Christ's words: 'a new commandment I give unto you, that ye love one another.' Love manifests itself on the moral side of Christianity in the sympathetic service of man, even to the sacrifice of self. As the guiding principle here is an attitude of mind, a code of laws can be dispensed with. But as guides to conduct the accepted moral standards remain, especially those expressed in the Ten Commandments of the Old Testament; a new moral content, however, is given to obedience to them by the new motive (love) which now underlies them all. This new motive evidently widens the range of morality. You remember that, in the history of most religious systems that range had gradually extended from the family and the kin-group to the tribe and even the nation. Two of them, Buddhism and Greek religion, during the latest phase, had actually begun to include other nations; but Christianity explicitly takes in the whole sphere of mankind: it is expressly universal. It does not, for instance, exclude its adherents from association with any other men by food prohibitions or by the seclusion of women. The neighbour here is not fellow-countryman, but fellow-man, and the fellow-man regarded as the child of the one Father over all.

It is not necessary for me to enumerate and classify the virtues recognized in Christianity, because they differ little from those that had been evolved in the later period of the various older religions I have surveyed. We should rather inquire what is the exact nature, according to the teaching of Christ, of the new and fundamental principle of love that is to govern morality, and how it is to be applied to the many moral problems of human life. The ethical system which Jesus found prevailing in his nation was both wide and deep. But by being bound up with religious worship and petrified in ritual observance, the morality of holiness had been transformed into something that was its exact opposite. Once when questioned as to what moral conduct consisted in, Christ answered: 'the sum of the law is, to love God and your neighbour.' He severed the connexion existing in his day between ethics and the external forms of religious worship. He would have absolutely nothing to do with what were called good works in combination with the ritual of worship. He was indignant with men who allowed their neighbours, even their parents, to starve, while they sent gifts to the temple. Love and mercy in his view lost all their value by being transformed into anything else than the service of one's neighbour: in other words the application of the principle must be in the service of man; the principle must be not merely an attitude of mind, but must be realized in the practice of human life.

Secondly, in all questions of morality, Christ goes to the root of action, that is, to the disposition and the intention. A large part of the so-called Sermon on the Mount is concerned with bringing out the disposition and the intention in each case, when he examines the several departments of human relations and human feelings. By them he judges a man's works, making heaven and hell depend on them.

Thirdly, when stripped of self-seeking and ritual elements, the moral principle is recognized by Christ to be one and one only, whether it takes the form of love of one's neighbour, of one's enemy, or appears as that of the Samaritan (who succours the distressed). But it is always the love that serves, this being the only function in which it exists and lives.

Fourthly, Christ applies this love, as an abiding disposition towards the good, in a spirit of humility.

In expressing his conception of the higher righteousness, as resulting from the new commandment of love with these four qualifications, Christ defined the sphere of morality as no one had ever defined it before. This can be realized best by studying the Beatitudes (' Blessed is he,' etc.) of the Sermon on the Mount. For these contain the essence of his teaching on ethics and religion.

Christ laid stress on mercy as the outcome of love, the quality on which everything depended, and on the temper in which it is exercised, as the guarantee of its value. Thus he said: 'Be merciful even as your Father in Heaven is merciful.' In his teaching God's justice is not accomplished by keeping to the rule 'an eye for an eye, and a tooth for a tooth,' but by the exercise of mercy.

This is the last step in religious evolution. It was an enormous advance in the history of religion. The previous stage reached was the idea of a righteous God, which through poets and thinkers in Greece, on the one hand, and through the Prophets in Palestine, on the other, had become a living force. The gods, on the one hand, were raised to a higher level and civilized, while the warlike and capricious Jehovah became a Holy Being. The Godhead had been moralized and was now 'holy and just.' The most immediate result of this development in the moral sphere could be summed up in the negative maxim: 'What ye would not that men should do unto you, do ye also not unto them.' This rule contained a civilizing force of enormous strength. Here the stage of justice, but only strict justice, had been reached. It may be expressed in the words: 'Be just.'

The last step was not reached till justice was compelled to give way to mercy, and the idea of brotherhood and self-sacrifice in the service of one's neighbour became supreme. Here morality was placed on a new basis. Its sphere could now be summed up in the positive maxim: 'What ye would that men should do unto you, do ye also unto them.' This is the advance made by Christ. It leads to the highest level of morality. It may be expressed in the words: 'Be merciful.'

Such being the general principle of Christian morality, we may now ask, what is its practical application to the great problems of life?

a. What is, in the first place, the attitude of Christian morality to the world? There is a widespread opinion, which is, in fact, dominant in the Catholic Churches, that in the last resort the teaching of Christ is a strictly world-shunning and ascetic creed. The Catholic Churches see a world-denying attitude in the Gospel, and teach accordingly that it is only in the form of monasticism that the true Christian life can be realized, that it is only monks that can follow Christ fully; though they recognize a 'lower' kind of Christianity without asceticism as 'sufficient.' This is almost exactly the attitude of Buddha. To the Russian writer Tolstoi, the leading feature of Christianity, is the shunning of the world; but the ascetic ideal which he derives from the Gospel includes the service of one's neighbour. Is then the Gospel of Christ a world-denying creed? There are certain passages which do not seem to admit of any other interpretation. Thus the answer to the rich young man: 'Go sell what thou hast and give to the poor, and thou shalt have treasure in heaven.'

Or the saying: 'If any man come to me and hate not his father and mother, and wife and children, and brethren and sisters, yea and his own life also, he cannot be my disciple.' Such passages seem to prove that the Gospel is altogether world-shunning and ascetic in its character. But let us consider the following points before deciding.

What was the manner of Christ's life? We find him saying, 'John came neither eating nor drinking, and they say, he hath a devil. The son of man (*i.e.*, Christ himself) came eating and drinking, and they say, Behold a man gluttonous and a wine-bibber.' From this it is clear that the impression made by his manner of life was different from that of John the Baptist, the ascetic preacher of repentance. We see Christ in the houses of the rich and the poor, at meals, with women and among children, and even at a wedding. He allowed his feet to be washed, and his head to be anointed. When he found people with a firm faith, he left them in the position in which they were: we do not hear of his telling them to sell all and follow him. He did not organize His disciples into a band of monks, or give them directions as to what they were to do or leave undone in the life of the day.

Again what effect had his teaching on his disciples? It is certain they did not understand their master to be a world-shunning ascetic. It is true they made sacrifices for the Gospel, and in a sense renounced the world; but it is evident that they did not make asceticism their chief aim. They did not send away their wives: we are told of Peter that his wife accompanied him on his missionary journeys. We find nothing in the apostolic age suggesting a community of men who were ascetics on principle. On the contrary, we find the conviction prevailing that a man's Christianity is realized within the calling and position in which he finds himself. How different all this is in the case of Buddhism from the very beginning. Christ speaks of three enemies with which mankind is confronted. He does not tell us to flee from them, but rather to overcome them: they are mammon, care and selfishness. By mammon he means enslavement to worldly goods. By 'care' he means timorousness in facing the future as opposed to trust in God, who preserves the very sparrows on the housetop. Against the third enemy, selfishness, Christ requires self-denial to the point of self-renunciation. It is not, however, to be met by any act of general renunciation, but by overcoming it. Against all these enemies what we have to exercise is self-denial, not asceticism, which maintains the theory that all worldly blessings are in themselves of no value. This is not the theory to which the Gospel leads. But there can be no doubt that Christ demanded self-denial and self-renunciation to a much greater degree than most Christians are apt to practise. But asceticism, as a general self-discipline, has no place in the Gospel at all. The kind of asceticism the Gospel means consists in the struggl against these three enemies, a struggle which serves ande is self-sacrificing. To a system, the leading principle of which is love, that serves one's fellow men, any other form of asceticism, such as monasticism, which is self-regarding and therefore anti-social, is essentially opposed.

b. What was the attitude of Christ as regards the constitution of society? He regarded the possession of worldly goods as a grave danger for the soul, as hardening the heart, entangling us in earthly cares, and seducing us into a vulgar life of pleasure. Thus he says: 'a rich man shall hardly enter the kingdom of heaven.' But it is certain that he never and nowhere wished to keep up poverty and misery; on the contrary he combated them himself, and bade others do so. It was only upon those who were anxious to devote their whole lives to the preaching of the Gospel and the ministry of the word that he enjoined the renunciation of all worldly goods. An absence of worldly possessions he required of the ministers of the word, that is, of missionaries, in order that they might live entirely for their calling. Missionaries and pastors have not as a rule followed Christ's injunctions to dispossess themselves of their worldly goods; and it is a question whether it would not have been a great gain to Christianity if they had followed Christ's rules. It does not seem fitting for one to preach resignation and contentment to the poor, who is well off himself. How can a man of property convince those who have none, that worldly goods are of no value? It certainly seems to me that such a position would be particularly ineffective in India because it is opposed to the Indian ideal of a religious teacher. With economic conditions and contemporary circumstances Christ did not interfere; for he was no social reformer. But no religion, not even Buddhism, ever went to work with such an energetic social message. How so? Because Christ applied the words 'love thy neighbour as thyself' with deep earnestness to all the concrete relations of life, to hunger, poverty, and misery, and because He uttered them not only as *a* religious, but *the* religious maxim. An illustration of this is to be found in the Parable of the Last Judgment, where the whole question of a man's worth and destiny is made to depend on whether he has practised love towards his neighbours. The tendency of the Gospel to union and brotherliness is its essential feature. The Gospel has prescribed no regulations as to how we are to use our wealth, but it leaves us in no doubt that we are to regard ourselves not as its owners, but as its administrators in the service of our neighbour. The Gospel is a social message of overpowering force; it is the proclamation of solidarity and brotherliness in favour of the poor. But laws or ordinances or injunctions bidding us forcibly to alter the conditions of the age in which we may happen to be living are not to be found in the Gospel. The Gospel of love is simply intended to adapt its shape to the course of history.

ρ. What was Christ's attitude to the constituted authorities of his time? His activities were in no way political; he was no political revolutionary, nor did he lay down any political programme. The way he understood his duty as Messiah is shown by his driving out buyers and sellers from the temple. In cleansing the temple it was not the constituted authorities whom he attacked, but those who had assumed rights of authority over the soul. In Palestine at that time the priests and Pharisees held the soul of the nation in bondage. For this unconstituted authority Christ showed an emancipating disrespect. He was never tired of attacking it, of exposing its greed and its hypocrisy. On the other hand, his attitude towards the real authorities, those who wielded the sword, was different. Recognizing that they had an actual right to be obeyed, he never withdrew himself from their jurisdiction. Thus he enjoined compliance with the demand for payment of the imperial taxes. When he said: 'render unto Cæsar the things that are Cæsar's and unto God the things that are God's,' he meant to say that the affairs of the soul have nothing to do with Cæsar, but belong to God. He held that the two departments must not be mixed up; the state must not usurp spiritual power, nor the Church usurp political power. Christ's opinion of the authorities as then constituted was that their functions were based on force, and for this very reason he put them outside the moral sphere. Not believing in the doctrine 'might is right,' he told his disciples to arrange their lives on an opposite principle: not to use force, but to serve.

Coming within the sphere of justice there are several sayings of Christ in which he directs his disciples to renounce all their lawful demands and so forgo their just rights: for instance: 'But I say unto you that ye resist not evil, but whosoever shall smite thee on thy right cheek, turn to him the other also. And if any man will sue thee at the law, and take away thy coat, let him have thy cloak also.' Such sayings have been taken to show that Christianity is incompatible with practical life. It is probably true that the strict application of this principle could not be carried out in those times nor even at the present day from the national or the international point of view. Are the magistrates, *e.g.*, not to inflict punishment, and thereby to efface themselves? Are nations not to fight for house and home when wantonly attacked? It must be remembered that Christ in his sayings did not speak in generalities, but always with reference to the individual case that came before him, in applying the principle of human kindness in society. In the family circle and in social life the practice of waiving one's rights is, it should be remembered, largely carried out. What family, what society, could continue to exist if every member of it were only anxious to insist on his own rights and did not learn to renounce them even when attacked? The attitude of Christ was based on the deep conviction that God does justice, and that, in the end, the oppressor will not prevail, and the oppressed will get his rights; and also on God's combination of mercy with justice by which he lets his sun shine on the just and on the unjust, a saying reminding one of the well-known Sanskrit verse: 'the moon withdraws not its rays even from the hut of the Chandāla.' Similarly Christ's disciples were to show kindness to their enemies and to disarm them by gentleness. They were by renouncing their rights to co-operate in forming a nation of brothers, in which justice was done no longer by the aid of force, but by free obedience to the good. Many men already pass through life by acting thus without having recourse to the strict justice of the law. Such should be the guiding star and goal of the historical development of mankind. Whether humanity will ever completely attain to it, is hard to say. But we can and ought to try and get near it, and at the present day, as was not the case a few centuries ago, there is a feeling of moral obligation in this direction.

IV. In this connexion the main principle of Christianity is of great importance. When science, art, labour, the progress of civilization become inspired by the love of one's neighbour, when a man feels that his work, of whatever kind it is, not being altogether satisfying because not an end in itself, becomes a means towards a great goal, the service of humanity, he must begin to be conscious that he is engaged in a noble task, well calculated to satisfy the aspirations of his soul. To enlist every man in this service for this purpose, should be one of the chief aims of Christianity at the present day. There is no healthy man or woman who cannot contribute his or her share to such service. The individual can do so in the family circle and in society by obliging and considerate conduct, by spreading sunshine, as it were, wherever he goes, with the aid of geniality and kindness. The rich man may contribute much to the alleviation of suffering and the amelioration of the social conditions of the poor by organized distribution of his wealth. The scholar by enlarging the boundaries of knowledge can increase enlightenment and thus remove some of the barriers that separate mankind. The man of science may by his researches produce inventions that save life in mines or on the sea; or, by discovering the causes of disease, cure and prevent an untold amount of suffering. The student of civilization may contribute to human progress by removing prejudices that result from irrational practices or customs surviving from early phases of society. The theologian may help to dispel religious misunderstandings or hatreds by showing how comparatively unimportant theological divergences are. Thus no one need be or feel a cumberer of the ground, but may be directed by a satisfying principle of conduct which serves as a guide through life, so that at the end of his days it may be said of him: 'well done, good and faithful servant, enter into thy rest.'

But the activity of the individual is not enough. There is at the present day an increasing recognition of the organic character of human society, of the dependence of all its parts on the whole, of the obligation of all the members to one another. The Christian morality of this age must, therefore, not only recognize fully the individual's obligations to others, but must also realize that many wrongs can be removed and many needs met, by common action alone. The social development of mankind requires the impulse and direction of a purposeful and voluntary co-operation. Foreign missions are the only form of organization which can deal with the situation produced by the contact which now exists between civilized nations and all the savage peoples. Otherwise this contact will result in the subjugation of the 'inferior' races to the ambition and avarice of the 'superior,' and in the moral deterioration of savage and civilized man alike.

It has long been felt that in the intellectual and social life of a single nation there are many things that can only be adequately done in the service of man by very extensive organizations, in some cases by the largest organization of all, the state. Here it may be said that the fundamental condition of progress is the systematic increase of knowledge, inspired by the love of man. A well-devised system of education, as applied in school and university, is of course the great instrument of enlightenment (*bodhi*), by which every man may ultimately be freed from the mental bonds of error that attribute the wrong cause to so many things.

A great deal in the way of education has yet to be done in the world as a whole. For it is only in a few countries of Western Europe and in North America and Japan that practically the whole population is able to read and write. In other civilized countries, only a small percentage (10 to 15) is literate; where the people are still savages, the illiteracy is, of course, complete. It is obviously of high importance that the education should be of the right kind. It makes, for instance, a great difference, even in primary education, whether it consists mainly in perpetuating traditional knowledge by the aid of memory, or in teaching even children to think and to know things by their causes, of course in proportion to their age and degree of intelligence. Otherwise, the judgment will be hardly trained at all, and the power of reading may only lead to the increased influence of wild and foolish agitators.

The present terrible state of Russia is a standing object-lesson of how a nation with a very low standard of education may fall a prey to the doctrines of fanatics.

Primary education must have a direct bearing on the needs of the masses; otherwise it may lead only to discontent and unrest. Again, the function of Universities in the true sense is not only to teach existing higher knowledge systematically and to train the intellect, but also to advance the boundaries of knowledge by research. This aspect of University work is peculiarly valuable in the service of humanity, not only by increasing man's conquest of nature, but by improving the physical and the mental well-being of mankind. It is unnecessary here to dwell on the wonderful practical achievements of great University chemists and physicists. But I must not pass over the immense benefits conferred on mankind by discovering the true causes of so many deadly diseases, and at the same time undermining a number of irrational beliefs. Thus every one has long been able to know that small-pox is much more effectively got rid of by vaccination than by prayers and sacrifices to an imaginary goddess supposed to send this disease. Medicine is the most philanthropic of all the sciences, able to do more than any other to alleviate human suffering. I do not know whether Indian students are entering upon the study of scientific medicine in anything like adequate numbers, but there is certainly no better way of enlisting in the service of humanity, and none giving so firm an assurance that a man has not lived in vain on this earth. The innumerable cases of heroism in saving life on the part of medical men during the late world-war was one of its few redeeming features. The immense advance in surgery resulting from that ghastly struggle is one of its few beneficial legacies. Even research in scholarship may result in world-wide enlightenment, drawing together widely separated branches of mankind. Thus the philological studies of Professor Bopp led to the proof that the different Aryan languages are related, that Sanskrit and English go back to the same origin, that the peoples speaking these languages are akin (though kinship on such evidence alone must not be exaggerated) and that all of them at one time professed different forms of the same religion.

The world had almost stood still in knowledge after the age of the Greeks till not much more than a century ago. Then natural science of every kind began to make immense strides in Western Europe, tending not only to increase human welfare, but to annihilate space and draw men together by multiplying and accelerating communications: by means of railways, steamboats, motors, aeroplanes, telegraphs, telephones, and perhaps the most marvellous of all, the wireless telephone. Thus within my own lifetime, I have myself experienced the voyage from India to England reduced from four months to a fortnight, scarcely one-eighth of what it was. Before very long the time occupied by the journey will be reduced to a week by aeroplane.

A striking example of the benefit derived from the organized application of science by the state, is to be seen in hygiene. The progress made in this department has already been great even in my lifetime. Thus when I was a boy the deathrate of London was about 22 per annum out of every 1000 inhabitants: it is now only slightly above 12. There seems to me to be an immense field for progress in this direction in India: not only in the promotion of health, but in the removal of prejudice and superstition. I remember several years ago being shocked at seeing in the report of one of the native States, the ruler of which took a special interest in medicine, that the deathrate there was 43 per thousand,

Such a rate of mortality could surely at least be halved by curing irrational methods of living.

The advance in the direction of humanitarianism has also been considerable during the last 100 years. A very serious social evil prevailed in the West Indies within that century, I mean negro slavery. This institution had become so repugnant to the spirit of Christianity, that the British Government, yielding to pressure, bought out the slave-owners of the West Indies for Rs. 300,000,000 in 1833. The example of England has been followed by all European countries in their colonies, so that no slavery now exists in the west, though it still survives in the Turkish Empire.

Till a comparatively short time ago harsh capital and prison laws lasted even in England. But it is quite certain that during the last century the conditions of human life, within the limits of nationality, have vastly improved in the west, largely owing to the influence of Christianity.

Till little more than ten years ago there had also been great improvement in the international relations of the peoples of the world. Since the appearance, in 1625, of the work of the great Dutchman Hugo Grotius on the Law of war and peace, the foundation of the modern science of the law of nations, a system of law unknown to the peoples of antiquity, had been growing up in the dealings between nations. It has its basis in community of religious views such as exist principally among European Christian states. It arose no doubt from the conviction that the level of conduct prevailing between nations (or states) should be as high as that applicable between individuals; as, for instance, the barbarous method of duelling to settle disputes has long died out among the most advanced nations, so international disagreements should not be decided by war, but by arbitration. And that, till ten years ago, its principles were considered binding as law, is proved by the fact that never in any published official act of the present age, verbal or written, has a state dared to declare that it did not consider itself bound by the law of nations and its principles. States have again and again solemnly declared their determination to abide by the principles of International Law. Thus in the Declaration of Aix-la-Chapelle in 1818, Austria, France, Great Britain, Russia, and Prussia solemnly stated that in forming this union they regarded as its fundamental basis their unchangeable resolution never to depart, either among themselves or in their relations with other states, from the strictest observance of the principles of the law of nations. In the negotiations for the treaty of London concerning the Black Sea in 1871, seven powers, Austria-Hungary, France, Germany, Great Britain, Italy, Russia, and Turkey, passed a resolution on the sanctity of treaties, stating that the plenipotentiaries recognized that it was an essential principle of the law of nations that 'no power can liberate itself from the engagements of a treaty, nor modify the stipulations thereof, unless with the consent of the contracting powers by means of an amicable arrangement.' This amounts to nothing more than what would be keeping an agreement between man and man.

Even in 1908, when Austria-Hungary proceeded to the annexation of Bosnia-Herzegovina, without obtaining the previous assent of the contracting powers who, under the treaty of Berlin of 1878, had granted her temporary occupation of the annexed provinces, the protests of the powers concerned were answered by Austria-Hungary declaring that she had done nothing contrary to the law of nations or against the sanctity of treaties ; for the powers had given, she asserted, their tacit consent to the practical transformation of her temporary into a permanent occupation. The public opinion of the civilized world plays, in an ever increasing degree, the part of a sanctioning authority. Successive diplomatic conferences have codified many of the chief branches of international usage : this diminishes the possible cases in which states can take advantage of the uncertainty of the law.

In 1856 the Declaration of Paris constituted the first actual enactment of rules of International Law. But the great work of reducing to writing the rules which had been floating as an unwritten law in the conscience of Europe was undertaken by the Hague conferences, which may be said to have created an entirely new factor in the domain of International Law. One of the conventions adopted in 1899 established methods for the pacific settlement of international difficulties, including the Hague Court of Arbitration. The work of the conference of 1907 was much wider and more exhaustive than that of 1899. It included a great many new conventions. Ten states took part in this conference.' The institution of the Hague Conferences had now provided a method of obtaining the consent of nations, not only to existing rules, but to their reform and to the introduction of new rules.

This immense advance had only been accomplished a few years, when the greatest war known to history broke out, instigated by a nation which had been trained for a generation in the doctrine that might is right, and that nothing else matters in international affairs. In this war that nation infringed all the most important rules of International Law, breaking the treaty of Belgian neutrality at once, bombarding undefended cities, sinking merchant ships and hospital ships indiscriminately, introducing poison gas, and inflicting atrocities on the non-combatant populations of Belgium and France. The one redeeming point in all this barbarism was that the Germans tried to make excuses by saying, for instance, that the violation of Belgian territory was a necessity, and that the sinking of non-combatant ships was in retaliation for the starvation of women and children by the British blockade, though they of course knew perfectly well that blockade is a universally admitted method of warfare, and that they themselves had reduced the whole population to the utmost extreme of starvation by the siege of Paris in 1870. It was still more difficult to excuse the ruthless submarine warfare, which was both barbarous and illegal. It has been a merciful dispensation that the champions of freedom, and not those of force proved victorious. Though international relations must suffer for a long time to come, especially owing to the intensification of nationalism or national vanity which since the war has arisen all over the world, nevertheless the foundation of the League of Nations, the greatest movement that has ever taken place in the direction of Universal peace, a movement to which 46 nations already belong, and of which all will probably before very long be members, must gradually lead to the world-wide realization of the doctrine of love as foretold in Tennyson's well-known lines :—

> When the war-drum throbs no longer and the battle flags are furled
> In the Parliament of man, the Federation of the World.

Selected Bibliography.

Harnack, *What is Christianity?* 1901; *Early Christian conception of Christ*, Engl. Tr., 1905; Fisher, *History of Christian Doctrine*, Edinburgh, 1896; Cairns, *Christianity in the Modern World*, London, 1906; Strong, *Christian Ethics*, London, 1896; Illingworth, *Christ and Civilization*, London, 1910; Gore, *Lux Mundi*, London, 1890.